Small Business Taxes & Accounting Guide:

LLC, Sole Proprietorship, a Startup and more - Learn How to Start and Plan a Business and Use Tax Deductions - Bonus: Quickbooks for Beginners & IRS Tips

By

Robert Schmidt

Table of Contents

Introduction...1

Chapter 1 – What Are the Business Entities Available?..................3

What Are the Benefits of a Business Entity?...........................4

Sole Proprietor...5

Limited Liability Company (LLC)..8

S-Corporation or S-Corp...10

C-Corporation or C-Corp...11

Partnership...14

Chapter 2 – Understanding Payroll Taxes..................................19

What Are Payroll Taxes?...19

Health Insurance and Retirement Plans................................21

State and Local Payroll Taxes...22

What Do You Have to Do Before Paying Payroll Taxes?...........24

Avoiding Common Payroll Mistakes......................................28

Is a Payroll Service the Right Option for Your Business?...........31

What is Involved in the Payroll Process - Calculations.......32

Chapter 3 – Understanding What An IRS Audit Means For Your Business..34

Why Is My Business Being Selected for an Audit?...............35

The Various Types of Audits..36

Why You Should Use Tax Professionals During Your Audit...............39

How to Prepare For Your Audit..41

What Can Potentially Trigger an IRS Audit...........................43

Survival Tips for Any Audit..46

The Outcomes of Your Audit..47

Chapter 4 – The Most Important Tax Deductions for Business Owners..50

What is a Tax Deduction for a Business?...............................51

What Are Ordinary Expenses that Qualify as Tax Deductions?..........52

What Are Capitalized Items and Depreciation?....................................54

Top Tax Deductions for Businesses....................................56

Chapter 5 – The Impact of the Tax Cuts and Job Act on Your Business..59

Corporate Tax Changes....................................60

Talking About Payroll Changes..........................61

Additional Benefits for Companies Creating Change.........................62

Other Business-Related Changes........................64

Conclusion...68

BONUS - Quickbook Guide

Chapter 1 – What is QuickBooks?..**71**

Targeted for Small and Medium Businesses.......................................71

Chapter 2 – No Matter Your Business, QuickBooks Can Help......76

QuickBooks Self-Employed..77

QuickBooks Simple Start..77

QuickBooks Simple Start, Essentials, and Plus..................................78

QuickBooks Pro Edition..78

QuickBooks Premier Edition...79

QuickBooks Enterprise Solutions...79

Chapter 3 – Basics for Navigating QuickBooks............................81

Adding and Searching for Data...81

Understanding the Financial Health of Your Business........................82

Tools for Determining Your Financial Health......................................83

Chapter 4 – Understanding Your Tax Liability.............................87

Tracking Business Expenses to Determine Deductions......................87

Estimating Tax Payments with QuickBooks..88

Chapter 5 – Options for Payroll and Timekeeping.......................92

Payroll Through QuickBooks Online..92

QuickBooks Payroll Services for Desktop Versions............................93

What Is Offered in the Payroll Service?..94

Time Keeping and Tracking Labor Costs..97

Chapter 6 – Deciding What is Right for You.................................99

Use QuickBooks to Apply for Financing..100

Determining What Is Right For Your Business...................................101

Introduction

It's an exciting time for you! Your idea for a business has grown to the point that you're ready to start making products or offering services. You are ready to open your doors. Hold on just one second! There are a few things that you need to make sure are in place before you switch the sign to open.

One of the most important aspects of any business is the foundation you create when you're first setting it up. That can provide protection to you as the business owner, but also give you the ability to have the benefits that come from investors or partners as your business grows. Those investors or partners can provide capital for the purchase of new equipment, the hiring of additional staff, and investing in software or technology to improve the processes of the business.

As you create an amazing business, there are going to be key areas related to your financials that need to be addressed. If you are not accurate in tracking your expenses and income, then you are likely going to have an inaccurate tax return. That lack of accuracy could end up costing your business in terms of time and money, as you deal with the interest and penalties relating to underpaid taxes at either the federal, state, or local level.

Therefore, as a business owner, you need to understand the financial rules that you are operating under for tax purposes. If you don't know them, then you are not going to be as accurate as you need to be in terms of your tax filings and deposits. Right from the start, your tax responsibilities are going to be based on the type of business entity you choose to operate under. Then your responsibilities continue to grow as you add employees and payroll taxes, plus the yearly income taxes that must be paid on the profits of the business.

If you are just starting out, then you clearly have questions about how you're going to set up your business and what to avoid in order to be successful right from the start. Those questions are going to be answered here throughout the next few chapters. Each one has a heading that reflects the tax implications covered in that chapter. You will be provided with a variety of tools and skills to assist you in taking your business to the next level.

The goal of this book is to share specific information that will help you choose the best means to set up your business. In particular, we are going to look at various tax implications based on the type of entity you choose for your business, as well as how to deal with the IRS in various instances, including if you are ever faced with an audit. The point is that you need to build a solid foundation for your business in order to be successful. Without it, your business may struggle to find success and will not be able to grow. After all, you are in business to make money and a stagnate business does not make money.

For anyone looking to start a business, it is critical to understand what types of business entities there are out there, what it means to set up payroll taxes, understanding the tax deductions available to your business and its industry, and even how to deal with the Internal Revenue Service, otherwise known as the IRS. Plus, we are going to dive into what the latest Tax Cuts and Job Act means for your business and give you some guidance on how to implement any changes for your company.

In the following chapters, you are going to learn about each of these areas, as well as some of the advantages and disadvantages that you need to be aware of throughout your journey of starting a business.

Chapter 1 – What Are the Business Entities Available?

When it comes to starting a business, you need to recognize the importance of setting up a business entity. While you may do business as a self-employed individual, having a business entity provides protection for your personal assets in a legal battle or if other issues arise.

A business entity is a separate legal being and that separation is what protects you from unlimited personal liability. Without the separation, your assets could be taken if an angry customer should receive a judgment against you. When you organize a business entity, then your liability is limited to what the state law determines is the liability of the business owners.

Setting up a business entity can be complicated, especially if you are not sure which one fits your needs best. Many individuals set up their business entity in such a way that it may make growth more challenging, simply because the entity might not be a good fit for that business and its long-term plans and goals. For instance, your business as a freelance writer providing services over the Internet will face different potential liability issues from the one that provides construction services to individuals in the local community.

Do you know what business entities there are available? A poor decision by a business owner regarding their entity may result from the fact that they do not know about all the options available to them. However, once you understand the options available, then it becomes easier for you to determine how you want your business structured to give it the ability to grow. It is key to understand that the type of entity you choose can impact how you exit the business or even how you pass it on to your heirs.

Regardless of the business entity that you choose to set up, it is critical to create a business plan. This will outline the operating principles of your business, along with the mission statement, goals for growth, and even an exit strategy.

Depending on the type of industry you are going to be working in, one type of legal entity may have greater benefits than another. There are a lot of factors that need to be considered when choosing the right entity for your needs. Throughout this section, I am going to focus on explaining what each business entity is, along with the benefits and challenges associated with each one.

What Are the Benefits of a Business Entity?

A business entity cannot protect you or your assets without being set up correctly from the start. Plus, if you do not properly maintain your business entity, then you are going to end up losing the protection that it affords your assets. The best entity for your business might differ depending on the type of industry that you are going to be involved in.

One of the biggest advantages of having a business entity in place is that you can now keep your personal and business assets separate. Doing so keeps your personal bank account and home from being used to satisfy any claims or judgments against the business.

Some business owners may opt to create several business entities to segregate their assets across several entities. For instance, an individual who is building a real estate portfolio may create an umbrella corporation, and then give each of his properties a limited liability company (LLC), which is owned by the corporation. It gives each property a legal entity, which can protect it from any legal claims against the other assets in his overall portfolio. There are a variety of ways that this can be used in a business, including separating different aspects of the business into their own entities. If you create promotional items for other companies, but also create your own promotional items to sell with your brand name, then each section of the business could be its own entity.

Another benefit of having a separate legal identity for your business is that you can start to build a credit history for your business. This process begins by establishing a legal corporate structure with all the fees and registration with the state. The next step is to get an EIN for your business, which can be obtained through the IRS. Then obtain the proper licenses for your business and keep your registration current.

Another aspect of the process is to obtain a Dun & Bradstreet DUNS Number. This is one of the major corporate credit reporting agencies and having a DUNS number is critical to applying for government contracts or to get a contract with a larger retailer.

Even with a number at a major credit reporting agency, you need to then have credit accounts opened in the name of your business. Choose companies that report to corporate credit agencies, because without those reports, your payment history will not be recorded. It is impossible to build a credit history without those regular reports.

Building a business credit history is similar to building your personal credit history with one notable difference. You need to make your payments early. Most commercial credit agencies look at payment history based on a shorter schedule than the traditional 30 days that reflects on personal credit history. The best way to earn a high credit score is to pay invoices on time or early if at all possible.

With a credit score for your business, you can then gain opportunities to access capital for periods of growth or even to expand your workforce before you try to capture new business. Plus, having access to a corporate credit history means you can expand into bigger contracts through the government and open up your market share immensely.

One of the final benefits of starting the process of creating a business entity is that you can enjoy tax benefits and higher income opportunities. Now that you can see some of the advantages of having a business entity, you might be ready to get one for your business. The question is which entity is the right one?

Let's start by discussing what business entity options are out there and the advantages or disadvantages of each one. Use these explanations to help you compare between the different options.

Sole Proprietor

A sole proprietor means that you are the sole owner and there is no legal distinction between the owner and the business entity itself. While you can employ other people, any profits will remain with the owner and will not belong to anyone else. There is the benefit that when your business is doing well, you are going to receive all of the profits after satisfying any tax bills related to the income or revenue received.

At the same time, it is important to remember that as the sole proprietor, you are responsible for all debts and losses incurred by the business. Your personal property can be seized or have liens placed on it to satisfy those debts. Every asset of the business is owned by the sole proprietor. While that means that you own business assets that can be sold to satisfy debts, you are also responsible for all the debt incurred by the business.

For those who are sole proprietors, that means you might find yourself in the position of having to sell personal assets to satisfy business debts if there are no business assets or if the business assets are not valued high enough to cover all the money owed. It does not provide the same legal protection for your personal assets as a limited liability company or a corporation.

Your business may have its own legal name or entity, as well as trademarks, depending on your county of residence, but again, these do not constitute a separate legal entity. Therefore, you can set it up to reflect the expenses and income received from the business, as opposed to other income received from different sources, such as investments, savings, or retirement plans.

There are several advantages to a sole proprietorship. The first advantage is that registering a business name for a sole proprietorship is fairly uncomplicated. The business owner may be required to register their business with various local governmental authorities. They will determine if the business name is a duplication of one that is already registered by another business entity. Once they complete that process, a business owner may be required to submit a form that allows them to acquire the title of DBA, which means "Doing Business As". The governing authority, which oversees this registration process, is known as the Secretary of State. However, depending on your state of residence, you may have a different governing entity to register with or to get a license to do business.

There is another benefit for married individuals. A permitted exception to the sole proprietor stipulation by the Internal Revenue Service (IRS) comes into play when the spouse of the sole proprietor works for the business. They are not classified as partners, thereby allowing the sole proprietorship status to remain intact.

Taxes for a sole proprietorship are paid through a Schedule C, which is then transferred into an individual's joint or single tax return. As a sole proprietor, you are responsible for paying all self-employment taxes and any other tax liabilities related to your business. However, since you and the business are considered one and the same, your business will not be subject to separate taxation. Instead, all the income made is considered the direct income of the business owner.

Although you can have employees under a sole proprietorship, it is important to understand that all legal responsibility for the decisions of the business belong to you. That also means you have unlimited liability for the actions of the business. As the owner, you are exclusively liable for all business activities conducted or completed under your sole proprietorship.

Here is how that might look in real life. You completed a project at a person's home and they were unhappy with the work or felt that the work related to the contract was not completed. If they sued you to complete or repair the work or pay for the completion or repair of the work, then the courts might side with them. That would mean you are now on the hook to pay for those expenses, along with the expenses related to your legal battle. It could end up costing you a significant amount, forcing you to liquidate your personal assets. Individuals have found themselves selling homes, cars, and other assets to satisfy these claims.

Others have even found themselves having to apply for bankruptcy protection as a result of claims against their sole proprietorship. While there is the benefit of being the only person who can make decisions for your business as a sole proprietorship, you can also see how it could have a huge financial impact should the business be sued or find itself in financial difficulties through a lack of cash flow.

Your business can also take advantage of small business loans insured through the Small Business Administration (SBA). As you grow your business, there may be other investment opportunities available, but if you are going to change the fundamental structure of the business, then you will have to make those changes legally.

Limited Liability Company (LLC)

An LLC is a private limited company that provides a pass-through means of allowing an individual to have the benefits of taxation as a sole proprietorship or partnership with the protections provided to a corporation. It is important to recognize that under state law, an LLC is not a corporation. However, it can provide legal protections to its owners.

When you use an LLC, then you benefit from the related flexibility. For instance, you can choose to run your business using corporate rules or the ones that govern a partnership. In some instances, an LLC can even be used to set up a non-profit. If your business will be providing professional services that need to be licensed by the state, then you may not be able to form an LLC. However, some states offer an alternative entity for those who must be licensed, known as a professional limited liability company (PLLC).

What are some of the advantages or benefits associated with an LLC? For starters, it provides protection to its owners by limiting the responsibility of the owner for the debts and assets of the LLC. Essentially, the LLC could be held legally responsible for its actions, but as the owner, you may not be required to put up personal assets to satisfy the debts incurred. Each state's shield laws may be different, so check with your state to determine how much liability you may have if the business were to encounter financial difficulties or were to incur legal liabilities.

Another benefit of an LLC is that you can still enjoy the pass-through aspects of a sole proprietorship with regards to taxation. It can be a flexible option for businesses that have one owner. In fact, ownership is often represented as membership, which can be distinguished from corporate shareholders.

One big advantage of an LLC is the ability to choose how to be taxed, either as a sole proprietorship, partnership, S corporation, or a C corporation. If you opt to be taxed as a partnership, you can lay out the members' distributive share of income, losses, deductions, gains, and credit through your operating agreement instead of using an ownership percentage.

Another benefit is that an LLC can have an unlimited number of members, plus those members do not have to be citizens of the United States. Since the LLC is a hybrid, it allows for some benefits associated with a corporation without all the administrative paperwork.

There are some individuals who argue that the best set up for a business is an LLC being taxed as an S Corporation (S-Corp), because that combines what makes an LLC attractive with the tax benefits associated with an S-Corporation. If your business is going to involve real estate investment, then you may find it beneficial to create a separate LLC for each of your properties, thereby protecting them from your main business, while protecting your portfolio from the dangers of cross-liability.

There are some disadvantages to an LLC, especially as you look to grow your company. One, the structure is more flexible and not governed by the rules and regulations that traditional corporations must abide by. Investors may be less interested in advancing funds to a business with less clearly defined rules and regulations that they must operate by, due to the increased risk they may incur.

Two, an LLC can be set up without an operating agreement. However, this can be problematic, making it difficult to address problems if the relationship between the members were to sour. Plus, you may find that the management structure is more fluid, which can make it difficult to get major initiatives completed, simply because you do not know who is in charge. Everyone may feel the need to make a decision and that can also make it complicated for your employees.

Depending on the state in which you set up your LLC, you may also need to pay a Franchise Tax or Capital Values Tax. These taxes are essentially the price you pay for enjoying the benefits of limited liability. Many of the states opt to determine your tax amount based on the revenue created by the business, an amount based on the number of owners, or an amount of capital determined by the state. Delaware, however, has chosen to employ a flat fee for this tax, which could make it an appealing option for setting up your LLC.

Renewal fees for your LLC can widely vary depending on the state. Plus, if you create an LLC with stock options, you may be required to publish an annual report. Other states can impose a publication requirement as part of the registration of your LLC, which can come at a significant cost to your business.

For a new business opting to use an LLC, it is important to set up your operating agreement at the beginning and clearly outline everyone's roles, along with how the business is going to be structured. Doing so will help to address potential problems and make your LLC more appealing to investors down the road.

S-Corporation or S-Corp

An S-Corporation, often known as an S-Corp, is a closely held corporation that does not pay any income taxes. The income or losses that come from the corporation, which can be set up as a partnership or a limited liability company, are divided and passed through the individual shareholders or members. That income or loss is reported on their tax returns.

The term "S" is understood to mean a small business corporation. As with a partnership, the income, deductions, and tax credits will flow to the shareholders annually, regardless of whether any distributions are actually made.

Your S-Corp is generally subject to the laws of the state where it is incorporated. Typically, a corporation is eligible to be an S-Corp if it meets the following criteria:

- Shareholders are individuals
- No more than 100 shareholders
- No non-resident shareholders
- One class of stock

To take advantage of the tax implications of an S-Corp, a limited liability company must first elect to be taxed as a corporation before making the S-Corp election under section 1362(a) of the tax code. The IRS does allow for late elections, but it is important to take care of this by the third month after the start of the tax year where you intend to file as an S-Corp.

I want you to note that the owners of an S-Corp are going to be taxed on their proportional share of the S-Corp, not what was distributed to the shareholders. Shareholders will receive a K-1, which they use as part of their tax return filing, which will list the income, losses, deductions, and credits that relate to their share. However, you need to note that a distribution in excess of the shareholder's basis is going to be taxed as capital gain. Shareholders may opt to pay estimated tax payments throughout the year to offset their potential tax liability associated with the S-Corp.

You may opt to transition your C-Corporation to an S-Corp, but you will likely also have to pay corporation income taxes on untaxed profits generated by the C-Corporation. For many businesses, the advantage of using an S-Corp is found in the fact that tax liability is shifted to the shareholders' individual tax returns. However, as your business grows, it can potentially outgrow the S-Corp status, thus requiring you to convert it to a C-Corporation.

If you are filing as an S-Corp, then it is strictly for tax purposes. Your partnership or limited liability company will still need to follow your operating agreement. If your business is a corporation filing as an S-Corp, then you will still be governed by the rules and regulations associated with your corporation and its industry.

C-Corporation or C-Corp

When you are deciding what type of entity to choose for your business, a C-Corporation or C-Corp can be a viable option to provide legal protection, as well as giving the owners the option to shift the tax burden for the corporation's income and losses to the corporation itself.

Corporations can be formed in all states, but the laws governing them can vary. They must issue a certificate of incorporation or formal articles of incorporation, as well as by-laws. There are generally no residency requirements, although a corporation typically needs to have one director and two officers. If you are the sole owner of your company, those three roles can be handled by one individual.

Recognize that your corporation is a legal entity, independent of you or your shareholders. Essentially, in the eyes of the tax laws, your C-Corporation is deemed a legal person, which means it can engage and create contracts, as well as be sued or sue others. Of course, that also means that your corporation must pay its share of taxes. Plus, as an individual legal entity, a C-Corporation will not cease to exist, simply because one or more of the shareholders have passed away.

When you set up your business plan and your exit strategy, you might see a C-Corp as the right entity to assist in your exit strategy or in the passing of your business to a family member as part of your legacy. Therefore, it is important to understand how your chosen business entity could impact your ability to pass your business to someone else within your family or to sell it as part of your exit strategy. Now let's talk about how your corporation's taxes are going to be calculated and what impact that would have on your ability to lower your tax liability.

In the past, your corporation would pay taxes based on a sliding scale, which reflected the amount of income and revenue the corporation generated. Starting in 2018, thanks to changes in the tax law, all C-Corporations are taxed at a flat 21%, regardless of their level of taxable income. Working with a professional tax accountant can help you to determine the best option to decrease the overall tax liability for your business and give you tax savings.

What are a few of the benefits of opting for a C-Corporation over another business entity? For one thing, corporations tend to be targeted less for audits by the IRS. That doesn't make your business audit proof. Since it has to file a separate return and is a separate entity, however, you are not necessarily going to be audited if your corporation is. To learn more about IRS audits and how to prepare for them, please review chapter three.

Another benefit is that as a shareholder, you have limited liability regarding the debts of the business. That means your personal assets are not likely to be used to cover the liabilities of the business itself. As a business owner, particularly one with employees, there are expenses related to the business that can be deducted by a C-Corporation. For instance, your business as a C-Corp could write off the costs of health plans established for your employees. Not only is it a business deduction, your employees are also enjoying a tax-free benefit.

Unlike with an S-Corp, which limits the number of shareholders to less than 100, a C-Corp can have an unlimited number of shareholders. If your business is in a period of growth, this ability will allow you to sell shares to potential investors and increase the capital available to your business. C-Corps can also raise funds through the sale of stocks. Plus, your investors do not have to fulfill any type of residency or citizenship requirement.

As the owner, known as the majority shareholder, you have the right to sell different classes of stock, such as preferred or common stock. Each of these types of stocks offer different types of dividend payments and other options. Additionally, these classes of stocks have advantages, depending on the overall strategy of the investor.

What is a preferred stock? It pays a fixed and regular amount of interest income versus a dividend payment. Preferred stockholders have a claim over a corporation's earnings and assets ahead of those who own common stock. However, their claims are behind those of bondholders and creditors. Depending on how you choose to structure the agreement under which you issue preferred stock, those who own it may have input regarding the operation of your corporation, may have the same input as common stockholders, or no input at all.

Common stock, on the other hand, provides voting rights and is considered equity capital of the firm. That means if the firm goes under, a common stockholder will not be paid back. When the corporation is struggling financially, a common stockholder may receive little or no dividend income from their stock. However, common stock does give its holder an unlimited proportionate claim to the assets and income of the firm behind the claims of the lenders and other obligations.

Clearly, a corporation can provide benefits during times of growth, while still allowing an owner to retain control. Investors are not lenders, so receipt of their funds in exchange for stock does not count as debt against the corporation, versus taking out loans to expand your business.

If that sounds appealing, you need to know what the requirements are to create a C-Corporation. Here are few of the key ones to keep in mind:

- Need to have adequate capital
- Formally issue stocks to initial shareholders
- Regular meetings of directors and shareholders
- Business records and transactions separate from owners' financials

It is important to remember that you cannot treat your corporation as an extension of your personal property, or you risk putting your limited liability protection in jeopardy. Other don'ts for your corporation includes:

- Do not personally guarantee a loan or business debt for the corporation, because you may end up liable for it if the corporation cannot pay it back.
- Do not fail to deposit taxes deducted from employees' wages.

Many individuals recognize that safeguards, including checks and balances through accounting, need to be in place to make sure that no fraud occurs. If fraud occurs, the individuals involved could be liable, and the corporation could be ruled as ceasing to exist by the courts. That would then remove the protections of a corporation for your business. Plus, when a court rules to end a corporation, there is usually evidence that the corporate formalities have not been adhered to during the course of doing business.

For an individual or a family creating a new business, these options all have pros and cons. However, what if you are looking to create a partnership, one that involves two owners, perhaps ones that have no other ties except through the business? Let's explore what a partnership looks like and some of the advantages and disadvantages.

Partnership

When you create a business partnership, you are essentially creating a legal relationship between two people. You are likely both pooling money or other resources, sharing skill sets, and sharing the ups and downs of owning and running a business. While a partnership can be a great way to gain access to capital or skills that you need, there are some things to keep in mind before creating a partnership.

One, you are going to share control of your business with another person. It is important to make it clear in your partnership agreement who has the final say regarding decisions relating to the business. After all, without a clear decision-making process, the business will flounder, and the employees will be confused regarding who is in charge.

As partners, you can structure your agreement to outline who works in the business and handles the day-to-day operations versus one who just consults on the larger goals and focus of the business. When setting up a partnership, you need to remember that unlike a corporation, your partnership is not a separate legal entity from the owners.

Secondly, a partnership can provide limited liability protection for its owners in the case of lawsuits or debts related to the business itself. Therefore, depending on the type of business you are creating, the liability risk needs to be factored into your decision regarding whether to go the route of a partnership.

When you are setting up a partnership, you need to be clear about what type of partnership needs to be created. There are three different options you can implement. The first is a partnership with general partners and limited partners. The general partners are the ones who participate in managing the partnership, and they are also liable for the partnership's debts. Limited partners, on the other hand, are more of an investor and often do not participate in the partnership's management.

The second partnership option is one where there are equity partners and salaried partners. The difference is that some of the partners may be paid as employees, but others only receive their ownership share of the partnership. This division is a way to pay the partner who is actually working in the business versus a partner that simply invests or puts equity into the business. You also need to define the decision-making process, especially if one partner is going to be working in the business.

The third option frequently used involves different levels of partners. For instance, you might opt to have a senior partner versus a junior one. What defines the difference between these levels will be outlined in the partnership agreement. Typically, there are different duties and responsibilities associated with each partner's level. Plus, a junior partner will not have the same level of input or amount of investment in comparison to a senior partner.

Now that you understand what your options are for the division of labor and responsibilities within a partnership, you need to know the types of partnerships out there. You may have heard of these types before, but here is a simple explanation of each one.

General partnership – This partnership is comprised of partners that contribute to the daily operation of their partnership, but they also have liability for the debts and lawsuits incurred by the business. There are no liability protections for the general partners, because they are considered legally the same as the business. You can easily create a general partnership, which typically have low operational costs and have few ongoing requirements for maintaining the partnership. On the other hand, they provide the highest risk to the partners, as they can also be responsible for the actions of the other general partners.

Limited partnership – A general partner manages the business and takes on the liability for the business. The other partners are limited, because they do not participate in management or incur liability for the partnership's debt. These are an option in cases where you are setting up a partnership for a short-term project versus running a business in the long term.

Limited liability partnership – In this case, you are combining the two previous partnership types. While you still have a limited partner or partners, there may also be more than one general partner. Using this option can help you to protect personal assets, but it does not shield partners from the liability for their own actions or malpractice.

Limited liability limited partnership – While this is not recognized in all states, the point is to provide protection for the general partners involved. It provides a greater shield from liability for them.

To form a partnership, you generally must register with the state that you are doing business in. It is important to note that the specific requirements for registration, as well as the partnership options available, will vary from one state to another. No matter how the responsibilities and ownership percentages work in your partnership, it is critical to lay everything out in a partnership agreement. This agreement will protect everyone by clearly defining what is to be done in various situations that impact the partnership. Too often, vague partnership agreements or a lack of one ends up causing problems for the business down the road.

Part of your agreement should include what happens if one partner wants to leave the partnership and another individual wants to join after the partnership has begun operating. You may set specific requirements for the incoming partner, including how much they must invest and how those funds will be used or handled. You also need to outline how much liability they take on and what their share of the profits or losses will be from year to year.

If you do not lay these things out in your agreement, then state law will determine how everything is divided, which could go against what you originally planned. I cannot stress enough the importance of having a written agreement. If you have questions regarding how to lay out your agreement, consider consulting with an attorney who specializes in these agreements. They can typically help you to cover the situations most likely to confront your partnership.

As you work on your partnership agreement, it is important to lay out the shares of the profits each partner will receive each year. The reason is that the partnership itself will not be taxed, but the partners will be. Partnerships do file an information return with the IRS, but the partners themselves will report their profit or loss on their personal tax return.

Partnerships tend to have more favorable tax treatment versus a corporation. It is important to note that corporations can be double-taxed, as corporate profits are taxed, as well as the dividends that are paid to the owners or shareholders.

Clearly, there are advantages to setting up a partnership. It is important to sit down with the individuals that are going to be a part of your business and discuss the goals of the business itself. This can help you to better define your partnership and make the right choice regarding the type of partnership you are looking to create.

I also want you to keep in mind that with each of the business entities discussed here, you are going to have advantages and disadvantages.

Find the one that gives you the most advantages for your particular situation. In order to be successful in business, regardless of the entity you choose, you need to create a business plan. As you create the business plan, be sure to include an exit strategy for the business.

What is an exit strategy? Simply put, it is the criteria that needs to be met for you to leave the business. That could mean reaching a certain profitability or value in order to sell or it may define when you will take on a reduced role. After all, you do not know everything about your business and may need to let someone else take over to see it grow to the next level. Others want an exit strategy because they do not plan on working forever. Exit strategies can also help you to define when you pass the business to the next generation.

The point of a business plan is to outline what the mission of the business is and where the business is headed. It can be changed or adapted as you and/or your partners see fit. However, a business plan serves as a guide for decision-making regarding the business. The reason it is so helpful is because it really outlines the mission of your business and the market you are going to be tapping into as you build up your business.

Your business plan will help you to determine which entity type is going to fit your needs, but you can also consult with business experts as you consider the pros and cons. The cost of that counsel from business experts can be money well spent to get your business off on the right foot.

Starting a business is not easy, but by understanding what you are in business for and how you want to set up your business, you can be successful. Now that you have decided what type of business entity you want to create and have done the homework for your state regarding registering your business entity, it is time to talk about how you get the work done and what tax responsibilities that entails. Yes, its time to talk about taking on employees.

Chapter 2 – Understanding Payroll Taxes

When you start your new business, you might be the sole employee, doing all the work in every area. Not only are you producing the product or providing the service, you are scheduling appointments, shipping out products, ordering inventory, handling the paperwork associated with the administration of the business, and so much more. When your business is young, you might be able to handle it.

However, as time goes on, your ability to handle everything can get stretched to the limit. You might have decided to take on an employee or several employees to help you handle the load of your growing business. However, that decision brings a new set of challenges, including how to handle payroll and payroll taxes.

Before you start the process of setting up your payroll, you need to understand what is involved in the payroll process, particularly as it relates to payroll taxes. The next few sections are going to focus on defining what payroll taxes are and what you need to know to set the right foundation for your payroll from the start.

What Are Payroll Taxes?

They are the taxes paid by employees and employers through the payroll process. According to tax law in the United States, you are supposed to pay taxes on your income as you obtain it. As an employer, you withhold these taxes for your employees, and send them onto the IRS and state taxation agencies on behalf of the employees and yourself as the employer.

Payroll taxes are used by the federal government to fund Social Security, Medicare, and other social insurance benefits provided by the federal government. Income taxes are used to fund various governmental programs, including defense and security. State income taxes are collected to fund education, health care, police, parks, and other items that help a state function.

To understand what is involved, it is important to know the various taxes that are typically withdrawn from an employee's check. Below are the main taxes that need to be withheld and how the amount of each employee's withholding is determined.

Federal income tax withholding – These are taxes withheld to pay federal income taxes owed by your employees. The amount you will be withholding is going to be determined by the W-4 form, which is filled out when they start working for you. An employee fills out their social security number, marital status, number of allowances, and any additional deduction amounts they want taken out of their check. As an employer, you are required to implement a new W-4 by the first pay period ending on or after the 30th day from the date you receive it from your employee. Now that W-4 remains in effect until the employee changes it, but once they do change it, the same timeframe for a new hire must be met. If you are going to issue bonuses and they want to change their W-4 in advance of that, give them time to make sure the changes will be implemented with that pay cycle. Keep in mind, a new or changed W-4 can only be accepted by being signed in person or through the mail. Put it into your new employee paperwork to make sure you have it signed by the employee and in your records.

FICA – These are the taxes being paid to Social Security and Medicare, otherwise known as the Federal Insurance Contributions Act (FICA). These are the taxes that are shared by employees and employers, with both contributing a portion of the amount owed. If you are self-employed or receiving income from a partnership or LLC, then you are going to be responsible for paying both shares to the various tax agencies. The employee tax rate for Social Security is 6.2% and that is the same for the employer. The Social Security portion is going to be capped each year at a maximum wage subject to Social Security. The employee Medicare tax rate is 1.45% and the employer tax rate is the same. In 2013, an additional Medicare tax was imposed upon individuals with higher incomes. This amount is 0.09% and is withheld from those who make over $200,000 annually. This tax is based on your employee's income level and filing status at the federal level. Medicare does not have a wage limit, so all your employee's wages and salaries are subject to this tax.

State income tax – These taxes will be paid into the state treasuries. However, there is only going to be a payment due if that state has an income tax. Currently, there are nine states that do not have income taxes, but that could always change. Therefore, you need to make sure that you understand your state's tax laws and how they want payments to be made. They also have their own payment schedule, so be sure to get that schedule and follow it. Each state may also have different rates and thresholds that you need to be aware of, in particular, how they apply to your business.

While these might be the major deductions, there are also the deductions that come from various benefits that you might offer to your employees. Two of these in the form of health insurance and 401(k) retirement plans are discussed below.

Health Insurance and Retirement Plans

Now you may also have to deduct funds for a health insurance plan offered through your business. This deduction must be taken before you take out their tax withholding for income, because these health insurance payments are considered tax-free by the government. Depending on the size of your business, you may not have to offer health insurance to your employees per the Affordable Healthcare Act (ACA). However, even if you are too small a business to be required to offer health insurance, you can still make it available to your employees.

On the other hand, if you are required to provide health insurance, then you should be aware of what types of insurance you need to offer. If you do not meet these requirements, then you risk a penalty when you file your taxes. Therefore, it is important to find out what your business is required to provide and the timeline for these provisions to be implemented. Doing so will help you to avoid any potential penalties related to this health care requirement.

Another payroll deduction that may come into play involves retirement funds. You may opt to make a 401(k) available as a benefit for your employees. Keep in mind that this deduction is also tax free up to a point.

Some 401(k) plans allow employees to make an additional deposit into their plan, but that deposit is going to come out of their check after taxes. Because they have paid the taxes on the income when it was earned, they will not have to pay taxes on it later when they withdraw it from the plan during retirement. Retirement plan deposits made under the tax-free option means that you will be paying the applicable income tax rate at the time you withdraw the funds from your retirement plan.

If you are creating a new business, then you have to decide the various benefits that you are going to offer your employees and what the criteria are for individuals to qualify and enjoy these specific benefits. Be sure that you clearly outline all of the criteria in your employee handbook, so there is no confusion as you start onboarding employees into your business.

As you can tell, there are a lot of moving pieces to calculate and track when you are processing your payroll, especially as it relates to the federal level. However, there are more taxes and withholdings that need to be accounted for at the state and local level. The next section helps to break down what you need to know about state and local taxes, as well as payments that need to be paid exclusively by the employer.

State and Local Payroll Taxes

Now that you have figured out the federal payroll taxes, it's time to talk about the state and local payroll taxes. First, you are going to have to calculate the state payroll tax based on the gross amount earned and deduct that. However, not every state requires that your employees pay state income tax. When you do not have to worry about state withholding for income tax, you reduce the number of places that you have to deposit funds and there are less dates to keep track of.

Some states also require that you withhold payroll taxes for unemployment funds, disability funds, and worker's compensation funds. These state payroll taxes apply depending on where your employees work, not necessarily where your business entity is registered. With a larger number of employees, you might find that payroll taxes require payments to several state and local agencies, not just the federal agency for FICA and income tax. It is important to create a system that allows you to keep track of all the dates and amounts owed for each state, as well as how they need to be paid. After all, some state agencies may have an electronic option, while others still require you to pay by mail with a certified check or money order, although some will accept a business check as payment. Never, ever pay your tax deposit with cash sent through the mail!

Employers have to pay some taxes that have not be deducted from their employee's paycheck but are determined in part by how much you pay your employees. For instance, you are going to have to pay Federal Unemployment Taxes (FUTA). The tax rate is 6% and is payable on the first $7,000 that you pay in wages to each of your employees during the year. Therefore, you need to be tracking how much you are paying to your employees, so you can determine who has reached that $7,000 limit and thus counts against what you owe to the federal government.

States also have a similar fund and the rate varies from state to state. They are meant to provide protection for your employees should you need to lay them off or reduce your staff due to a decrease in your level of business. However, if you pay your state unemployment taxes (SUTA) on a timely basis, then you can receive an offset credit of up to 5.4%. Again, the importance of being timely with payments is key to benefiting from this credit and avoiding potential penalties. Therefore, be sure to find out the dates these funds are due, and the amounts required by the state that your business is registered in.

One of the items payable on payroll that has become more common are taxes for cities and counties. These are often referred to as local taxes and can be required depending on where an employee lives. That being said, your payroll taxes can be complicated if you have employees that live outside of the state where your business is registered. When you find out where an employee lives, then it is important to determine what local taxes may need to be withheld.

You should always check with the local government agency to determine if any local taxes need to be paid and how those taxes need to be deposited. Not every state and local institution has an electronic option, but many do, and they may prefer you make your deposit using that means. However, if you are required to mail it in, then you need to find out if there will be a penalty if it arrives late. Some government agencies will credit you based on the date it was postmarked, but not all of them will do so.

What Do You Have to Do Before Paying Payroll Taxes?

As part of the process of paying payroll taxes, you need to acquire a Federal Employer Number (EIN). This number will allow you to file payroll taxes with the government, and make sure that they are credited properly. Essentially, this also becomes the equivalent of a social security number for your business. Once you complete the process of receiving your EIN, then you can set yourself up on the government's website to use their electronic payment option.

Today's electronic options allow you to see a credit to your account and confirm that the government received your payment right away. Those confirmations are key if there is ever a question regarding the amounts paid to the IRS for your business and employees. Do not assume that it is not necessary to keep those records, as errors can occur, and your records could assist you in avoiding penalties later.

The IRS requires that you use their EFTPS Online System to make your deposits. When you are first starting out, you need to go to https://www.eftps.gov/eftps/ to register your business and then you can start making your deposits, which can be deducted right from your business account. The IRS does offer some assistance when dealing with the EFTPS if you have any questions or challenges during the process. Recognize that you cannot mail in payments, because deposit coupons no longer exist, and the IRS is no longer accepting payments via this method.

The IRS determines when your payroll taxes need to be deposited based on an employer's total gross Social Security/Medicare liability for a 12-month period ending on the most recent June 30, which is known as the look-back period. The payroll deposit schedule is mostly based on the amount of payroll taxes you owed in the past. That being said, many employers opt to make their deposits as each payroll occurs to be sure they meet all required due dates. Thus, they are depositing that payroll's taxes right away, instead of holding them until a specific date. After all, if there are technological glitches at any point, you do not want to have the problem happen on the same day your taxes need to be deposited.

Additionally, you will need to file a payroll tax report quarterly using a Form 941. These forms typically need to be filed on a quarterly basis, according to the IRS schedule. Your state may also have specific filing requirements that you need to fulfill as part of your state payroll taxes. As a business owner, you are responsible for meeting the requirements of the state that your business is registered in, as well as any require-ments from the states where your employees live if it is a different state from the one that they work in.

Certain states have reciprocal agreements regarding the income tax being collected for individuals who live in one state and work in an-other. By finding out what the reciprocal agreement might be for the states surrounding you, especially if you are doing business close to a state border, you will be prepared for any additional requirements that may be imposed upon your business.

These reciprocals agreements are most likely found in the East and Midwest, although Montana is one exception. As a worker in a recipro-cal state, an employee can fill out the state's exemption form and pro-vide that to their employer. Then as the employer, you do not have to withhold taxes for their work state, but you can withhold taxes for their resident state. However, as an employer, you are not obligated to with-hold income taxes for your employee's resident state. By doing this for your employees, you are helping them to avoid underpayment penal-ties when they file their state tax forms.

Why do states create these reciprocal agreements? Essentially, they are meant to relieve the taxpayer of the burden of paying income tax in two states. Thus, they don't have to file to receive credit in their work-ing state that they would then have to apply to their resident state tax li-ability.

To be clear, all these withholdings and their deadlines, both for de-posits to be made and forms to be filed, need to be handled as a high priority when completing your payroll. If these deadlines are not met, then your business could be subject to significant fines. These start at 2% of the past-due amount if your payment is up to five days late. After that, the penalty goes up to 15% if you are past 10 days of non-payment and the IRS is forced to send you a payment notice. Clearly, it is critical to make sure that payroll tax deposits are made on time. If the IRS feels your business has willfully avoided paying your payroll taxes, then you may run the risk of jail time for tax evasion, which can be up to five years and include a fine of up to $500,000.

There are other penalties that can be assessed from state and local government agencies for non-payment of state income taxes or non-payment into SUFA. However, there are not just penalties for non-payment. You can also incur penalties if you do not file your quarterly return on time, if you do not file your monthly Form 941, and if you forget to submit a W-2 for any new employee.

A critical point is that the IRS is going to be focused on enforcing the payment of withholding and social security tax fund payments. As a result, the penalties for non-payment of these taxes is more severe. By more severe, I mean that you could be charged a penalty of up to 100% of the unpaid amount due from a company or the individual who is in charge of making the payments for that company or business.

When you are making a deposit for your payroll taxes, there are three components that are part of a correct deposit. These include that the deposit is made on time, in the correct amount, and that it was made in the correct manner. If you take care of all these components, along with the correct forms, then you are going to be one step ahead in the area of payroll taxes.

For those that opt to make your payroll deposits without using a payroll service, the next few paragraphs focus on the deposit schedule that you will need to follow as determined by the IRS. It is important to be familiar with this schedule to avoid the penalties mentioned above, as that can impact the financial well-being of your business. Therefore, creating a process for managing payroll is key to making sure all the taxes are paid promptly to the right agencies.

If you are a new business and have no look back period, then you will be making monthly deposits. Employers, who have a payroll tax obligation of less than $2,500 per quarter or total payroll taxes for the look back period of $50,000 or less, will be required to make a monthly deposit. That monthly deposit will need to be done by the 15th of the following month. For example, your payroll taxes for March will need to be deposited by April 15th to avoid any penalties.

Those employers with a total payroll tax obligation of more than $50,000 will be required to make their payroll tax payments on a semi-weekly schedule. How does that work? It will depend in large part on when your payroll is paid. The schedule is included below:

Payrolls paid on Saturday, Sunday, Monday, or Tuesday must have taxes deposited by the following Friday.

Payrolls paid on Wednesday, Thursday, or Friday need to be deposited by the following Wednesday.

Tax obligations of more than $100,000 must be deposited by the next day after payroll is paid and that requirement will be in place for the rest of the year and the following year as well.

The IRS also has a few rules to keep in mind in light of the fact that deposits may be due on days where banking is not available. For instance, if your due date is on a non-banking day, such as a weekend, then you will not be charged any late fees if it is paid by the closing of the next banking day. Thus, if your deposit was due on a Saturday, then you have until the close of business on Monday to make the payment without it being late. This system also works when a federal holiday closes the banks.

Semi-weekly depositors are given three banking days following the close of the semi-weekly period to make their deposit of any taxes withheld and accumulated during that period. Your business receives that small grace period, but you need to make sure your procedure is in place to avoid exceeding that grace period.

If you make a deposit error, you are not going to be penalized if the error does not exceed $100 or 2% of the amount that you are required to deposit. However, if you want to avoid any penalties, the balance due must be made up by a pre-determined make-up day. If you have not made it right by then, you are going to incur penalties based on the amount owed. Again, a payroll process being in place is key to avoiding these penalties. However, the later you are in making your deposit, the greater the penalties. Once a deposit is 15 days late, then you are going to face a 10% penalty. There is also a 10% penalty if you make a payment but do not use an electronic funds transfer (EFT).

Once the IRS starts sending out notices, then you have to deal with additional penalties. For instance, if you have unpaid amounts more than 10 days after the date of the first notice requesting the payment of the taxes that are due, then you are going to be accessed a penalty of 10% for those amounts and an additional 5% for the fact that the taxes are still late. Can you see how quickly those costs can rise and negatively impact the cash flow of your business? To avoid having these issues, you need to create procedures and processes to protect the financial well-being of your business. These processes can also help you to avoid an audit, which will be discussed in greater detail in the next chapter.

You also want to make sure that you put a policy in place to allow for training of the individuals who handle your payroll. Continuing education will help to make sure that they are doing their calculations correctly and to make sure they understand any changes in the tax law that could impact your business and its payroll. Clearly, there is a lot that goes into the process of handling payroll, especially as your business continues to grow.

Avoiding Common Payroll Mistakes

When it comes to payroll, there are a variety of common mistakes that you can make, which can put you in the position of having to deal with some of the problems that I mentioned above. In this section, I want to focus on what those mistakes are and how to avoid them in your business.

One of the first and most common mistakes is setting up your payroll incorrectly. Essentially, if you do not set up the foundation of your payroll correctly, then you are going to cause yourself problems and it will often be difficult to correct them. Payroll taxes can be complicated and as we discussed earlier, you need to make sure that you withhold the right amounts from everyone's paychecks and understand how much you need to pay as well. There are plenty of resources out there, so take advantage of the online resources from the federal, state, and local government to make sure that you get your payroll set up right from the start.

Another option to make sure you get off on the right foot is to consider using a payroll service or hiring an accountant. I will be discussing a payroll service in greater detail in the next section.

The next common mistake is one that we have already discussed, but bears repeating. Your tax payments need to be on time. Late payments mean penalties and accrued interest, which can be a financial blow to your business. Plan ahead and register your business before taxes are due so that you already have the necessary identification numbers for your federal, state, and local payroll entities. That will help you to avoid having any late payments.

The next common mistake is not calculating overtime properly. Under the Fair Labor Standards Act (FLSA), you have to pay people premium for their overtime hours. Calculating overtime gets tricky, because you also have to follow state and local wage and hour laws, especially if they could be more favorable for your employees. Then there are the daily overtime and double time rules as well. Take advantage of the guide provided by the Department of Labor to help you navigate the calculations related to overtime for your employees.

Another problem that frequently happens with payroll is that you run that payroll too late. After all, you are a busy business owner and you have a lot of demands on your time. It can be easy to lose track of what day it is and then be scrambling to make sure that your employees are paid on time. Forgetting to process their checks can lead to potentially costly mistakes but also some pretty unhappy employees. You might end up over or under paying your employees, because you are rushing to complete the payroll processing. Then you have to take the time to make the corrections and even pay the fines associated with payroll taxes. Clearly, these issues can be avoided by putting your payroll into a system or using a special payroll service to make sure that you meet all the deadlines.

At this point, I need to point out that if your employees quit or get fired, you have a specific amount of time to give them their last paycheck. To know what the timeframe is, you need to check with your state and find out what they require. Even if you are not planning on losing any employees in the near future, you want to be familiar with the rules and be prepared to execute them.

Are you keeping good records? Many business owners trip up by not keeping accurate records of their payroll. What is funny is that many of these businesses are keeping meticulous financial records in all other areas of their business, yet they seem to fall down when it comes to payroll. You are required to keep your payroll records for at least three years and your state may require you to maintain payroll records for a longer period, depending on whether the state has such a requirement. Again, you need to check with your state to find out what they have determined is the length of time you must keep these records.

The state's requirements will also determine what information you need to keep as part of your records. For instance, your state may require you to hold onto the I-9s, W-4s, timesheets, and payroll files along with copies of the tax forms, employee pay stubs, and more. Setting up a procedure to close a month or year of payroll can make sure that all your records are kept organized and keep you in compliance with your state requirements.

In line with poor recordkeeping, bad bookkeeping is another problem facing businesses when it comes to their payroll. By putting procedures and processes in place, you can avoid the consequences of bad bookkeeping. However, you might also opt to hire someone to handle your bookkeeping for your business, either outsourcing it or hiring a person for the sole purpose of handling your financial records.

As you can see, there are a variety of areas that can impact your payroll and make it a complicated area in the process of taking care of your business. Therefore, you might be asking yourself as a business owner, do I have any other options to handle payroll? Well, the truth is that you do have another option, which I will discuss next.

Is a Payroll Service the Right Option for Your Business?

All these dates and schedules can make the payroll process more complicated. After all, you are also trying to run a business. Many businesses are now taking advantage of various payroll software systems or services to handle the process of paying their employees, depositing their payroll taxes, and also handling any tax filings as part of the process.

It is important to keep in mind that if you choose to use a payroll service, there will be additional costs related to that service, which are typically required to be paid when each payroll is being handled. Therefore, you want to make sure that you calculate the costs before you decide on a service.

After all, if you have multiple employees and the time it takes you to complete the payroll is significant, then the cost of the service might be worth the effort. Other businesses with just a few employees might find it easier to use software and complete the payroll process themselves. Your time as a business owner is valuable, so you need to determine what is the best use of your time and energy.

Business owners might conclude that the cost of handling these administrative tasks is higher than the cost of a service because the use of their time means lost sales and less time for customer service. Recognize too that as your business grows, you might need to opt for a service where in the past you might have been able to handle the process on your own. However, there are other options that can allow you to keep the payroll process in house while keeping the costs budget friendly.

Payroll software can be a way to compromise the cost of a payroll service against the value of your time and energy. Using software, you can make calculations easily and determine how much you owe in tax payments, as well as completing your tax reports and filings.

What is Involved in the Payroll Process - Calculations

Clearly as your business grows, you might want to delegate the payroll process to another individual within your business instead of continuing to use a payroll service. Therefore, it becomes prudent to hire or promote an individual to handle the process of calculating payroll and taking care of the depositing of your payroll taxes. Again, it all depends on the size of your business and if that decision adds value.

As your business grows and changes, you will find that your original processes may need to change. Plus, you want to make sure that whoever is handling your payroll is using the right calculations to deduct the correct amounts. As I will discuss in chapter five, recent changes to the tax laws through the Tax Cuts and Jobs Act have meant that employers will have adjustments to make in the payroll process. While there may be changes that you have to make in processes or calculations, you may also see benefits, depending on your business or industry.

So just how are payroll taxes calculated? First, as the employer or the person designated by the employer, you calculate how much your employee earned for the pay period. Typically, that is determined by taking their hourly salary and multiplying it by the number of hours worked. If your employees have overtime, then you will need to determine the number of overtime hours and calculate that against their overtime rate, whatever that may be.

Once you know their gross pay, then you will have to calculate the specific amount to be deducted based on the information from their W-4 and the amount due for FICA taxes. Both of those amounts are to be deducted, along with any pre-tax deductions, and then the final amount is paid out to the employee. As you complete the calculations, you must make sure that you also deduct any state or local taxes.

Throughout the process of calculating the individual tax withholdings, you also need to figure out how much you owe as the business for these taxes. These deposits are also going to need to be made in a timely manner to avoid penalties. Throughout this chapter, I have introduced the various aspects of payroll taxes, but I have also continued to stress the importance of timely deposits. Penalties can grow quickly and become a financial burden for your business, and they are best avoided.

Now that we have discussed the importance of paying your payroll taxes on time, it is time to discuss the various steps a business needs to take in order to limit the chances of being on the receiving end of an IRS audit. Additionally, it is important to know what to do if you are ever faced with an IRS audit.

Chapter 3 – Understanding What An IRS Audit Means For Your Business

Filing your taxes and keeping records are just a few parts of the administrative duties that help to keep your business running smoothly. In fact, tracking your finances, including income and expenses, can be part of the daily routine. As the business owner, the health of your business can be found in the numbers that you are recording in your financial software. Therefore, you are constantly checking and analyzing the numbers to understand where your business is thriving and where you might need to address weaknesses.

At this point, you need to have a written policy in place that outlines your accounting procedures, as well as the checks and balances that you have in place to avoid potential mislabeling of expenses. Having this policy in place can help you avoid various situations that could potentially trigger the IRS to conduct an audit, as we will see below.

The IRS has the right to audit your business returns for up to three years, so they can go back across several returns. Businesses are encouraged to keep seven years of tax returns. However, if you make a habit to keep them, then you open a door for the IRS to audit further back. It is important to set up a system of destroying or shredding your oldest tax returns once the new one has been placed into your records. Demonstrating this is and continues to be your normal business policy can help to limit how far the IRS goes back into your records for a potential audit.

Therefore, with all the work you do to manage your books and to make sure you have tracked all your expenses, including receipts and invoices, it can be a surprise to receive a letter from the IRS indicating that you are about to be audited. For a majority of individuals, their vision fills with an examiner in a room, going over every piece of your accounting for years, searching for mistakes and deductions you shouldn't have taken before you end up having to pay a ridiculous amount of money in both a tax bill and penalties. It can seem terrifying, but the reality is that most audits are nothing like that scary experience we have built up in our heads.

So, what exactly does it mean to be audited by the IRS? Here are some answers to the most frequently asked questions relating to this topic and ways that you can minimize the chances that your business will end up on the IRS audit list.

Why Is My Business Being Selected for an Audit?

An audit is essentially an objective independent examination of your financial statements or, in the case of the IRS, an independent examination of your tax filing and the related documents. The IRS is naturally looking to make sure that you have filed your return correctly and accurately. Most businesses and personal returns aren't going to be pulled for audit. In fact, the IRS pulls less than 2% of returns overall for audit. That means your business has a very low chance of being audited, although that chance appears to increase the greater the taxable profit that your business produces.

The first point that needs to be made regarding this topic is that just because your business was selected to be audited, it does not mean that your business has done something wrong or that you made a mistake in your filings. It could simply be that your deductions or another part of your return were outside of the norms or parameters that the IRS has set, as you will see below. Part of the reason that certain individuals and businesses get pulled for audit is due to several methods the IRS uses as part of their process to make sure returns are valid and accurate:

Random Selection and Computer Screening – The IRS may reject a return based solely on various statistical formulas. Essentially, they are comparing your return to similar ones and preselected norms. If your business return appears to be outside of those norms, then it may get pulled for audit.

Related Examinations – Your business return might be selected if it is related to another taxpayer's return and they have some issues. For instance, there may have been an issue with your partner or investor's return, so your business return may have been pulled for audit as well. Since we have focused on the various business entities in chapter one, you can see how easily returns can end up being connected and cause a chain reaction of audits.

Once your return has been selected, it will be reviewed by an experienced auditor, who may opt to accept your return without any further questions. However, if they find something that they deem questionable, then the examiner will note those items and send the return onto the examining group for further processing.

If you have filed an amended return, that doesn't mean the original return will not get pulled for an audit. Additionally, your original return might not have gotten pulled, but your amended one may be pulled for an audit. Once your return has been selected, the IRS will notify you in the mail. They will never initiate an audit with a phone call, so if you receive one, then you should probably be suspicious about giving them personal information regarding your business and its finances.

Once you receive the notification, then you are likely to need to correspond with the IRS through the mail or a scheduled in-person interview, where the examiner will review all the records related to the return in question. The process is going to involve questions and reviews, but in the end, you may find that everything is completed with no changes to your return. It is important to not volunteer additional information, as if you do, then you could potentially extend the audit.

Now you might be wondering what types of audits there are and how they could potentially impact your business. Along the way, I will also share with you the importance of considering professional help to deal with your audit.

The Various Types of Audits

The audit done by mail is probably the easiest and usually allows you to resolve everything with just a few letters back and forth with the IRS. However, there are other types of audits that require more work from you. The first of these is the in-person interview, which can be held in a variety of locations. The point of an in-person interview is to provide specific information but to also answer questions related to the return in question.

No matter where the in-person interview is being held, be it your office or your accountant's office, the IRS will provide clear instructions and contact information necessary. Now that you have received the request for an audit, you need to start preparing for that audit. However, if you need more time to respond, it is important to fax a written request to the number on the letter that you have received from the IRS. You may receive a one-time automatic 30-day extension, but that is typically the only extension that you will receive.

If your request is denied, then you will be notified by mail. A Notice of Deficiency, which is received through certified mail, will automatically mean that you cannot have an extension for submitting the requested supporting documentation. Part of the reality is that the IRS expects you to respond within a specific time because you are supposed to keep all the information related to your return together with the return.

While a majority of audits are going to be handled through the mail or even an in-person interview, there are a few other audits that demonstrate an increase in IRS scrutiny. The first is an office audit, where you are asked to come into the local IRS office and bring in specific requested documents. For this type of meeting, you may consider bringing in your accountant to help you answer any additional questions that may come up during the audit.

A field audit, on the other hand, has the IRS coming to your office to examine documents and conduct an audit in person. As a result, this type of review can get more in depth, but it is also a time for you to demonstrate that you have all your related documentation for each of your tax filings, especially those that are being questioned by the IRS. It is recommended that you have your accountant and a lawyer present during any type of field audit.

The final type of audit is the Taxpayer Compliance Measurement Program Audit, which is an intensive review, because all the aspects of your tax return will be examined, not just the items that may have raised a red flag or potential compliance issue with the IRS. This type of audit is going to require that you have all the documentation for your return, but also additional documents related to information on your return, such as marriage and birth certificates. From the IRS point of view, this type of audit is meant to help update the data used to write the programs the IRS uses to scan and accept returns that are filed electronically. As with the field office audit, it is important to have your accountant and lawyer present for this audit.

Once the reason for the audit and the type of audit that you are going to be dealing with is made clear, then you need to start the process of combing through your records to produce the correct documents to back up the information within your tax return. This process includes providing the relevant receipts and documents that prove the validity of your deductions, income, or losses.

It is important to remember that you should never send an original document or your only copy of a document to the IRS. Send in copies or make a scan to submit it electronically if possible. While being nervous about an audit can make you want to overshare to prove that you didn't make a mistake on your return or attempt to defraud the government in any way, it is important that you don't overshare. Simply give the IRS what they have asked for and nothing extra.

If you are gathering documents and realize that something is missing, you need to request duplicates immediately. The IRS is not going to accept you telling them that the records are lost or missing. If you can't produce what they are asking for, then they will adjust your return and it may not end up going in your favor. However, once you have all your documentation together, make sure that it is organized.

Doing so will make it easier for you to provide what is necessary for the request and then if additional backup is requested, you can easily access it without panicking. Plus, that good organization shows that you are a responsible taxpayer, one who is trying to do the right thing. That good representation of your position as a taxpayer could result in the agent limiting the scope of their investigation, which can decrease the chances of your business having a large tax bill to pay as a result of the audit.

Why You Should Use Tax Professionals During Your Audit

Finally, depending on the scope of the audit, you may consider getting a tax lawyer. This type of attorney can help to protect your rights during the audit, but also assist you in making sure that you do not make a mistake that ends up costing you time, money, and potentially time in jail. The tax lawyer will understand the tax laws that are relevant to your audit. They know how to handle various situations that could come up.

Here are a few of the benefits of hiring a tax lawyer for your IRS audit, in addition to having your accountant or CPA present.

1. If you find that your business is in significant trouble with the IRS, then you want to have someone on your side who can advise you without later being forced to testify against you. With a tax attorney, you will have the benefit of attorney-client privilege, which means you can share with your attorney, but they cannot testify against you in court at a later date.

2. Your tax attorney will be able to assist you in reaching a tax settlement if you are found to owe the government. While your accountant or CPA may have some familiarity with the various tax settlement options available, they are not going to have the information regarding the ins and outs of the various programs that could apply to your situation. There are also a variety of tax codes and laws that change almost annually, plus they can be extremely complex. Programs available to troubled taxpayers can help you to reduce or settle the amount of tax debt you may have as a result of the audit, so you need someone who understands your situation. They can then help you to determine what programs you qualify for, as well as help you determine which is the best for your situation.

3. If you are placed into collections with the IRS, it can be a difficult time. With the wrong advice, you can make errors that have long-term financial implications. A tax attorney can help you to

navigate this situation, thus keeping you from a negative impact on your financial future.

You also need to notify the individual who prepared your tax return. Your preparer can help walk you through the audit process, but they can also help you to answer any questions based on the actual return, since they helped to put it together. The point is to provide protection for you and your business by bringing professionals who can guide you through the process.

There are also deadlines that impact the amount of your penalties. Missing them means you run the risk of your bill with the IRS growing. Plus, poor lines of communication with the IRS can negatively impact your ability to reach a resolution to the issues found on your tax return. Having a tax attorney can benefit you because they often have direct contact with the necessary branches of the IRS. After all, you don't want to try to reach a settlement or negotiate with the wrong department. Plus, a tax attorney can often do that negotiation over the phone versus in writing, so any miscommunication is limited.

Another reason to use professionals when dealing with an audit is that they can help you to negotiate an offer in compromise, which is an agreement between a taxpayer and the IRS to address the tax liabilities without paying the full amount owed. Essentially, you are offering them a set amount to consider the entire balance settled.

This repayment option could be a viable choice if you are:

Not able to pay the full amount in a reasonable time, either via a lump sum or a payment agreement.

In doubt regarding the amount of your tax liability, although this is a rare case and not likely to apply to your circumstances.

Dealing with exceptional circumstances, where if you were to make the full payment, it would cause an economic hardship.

The reality is that if you can set up a payment plan, the IRS is more likely to accept that versus an offer of settlement. The reason is that unlike creditors, who have limited options to collect their money from you and are thus willing to take a smaller settlement amount versus getting nothing at all, the IRS has multiple options available to collect their money. They can take your refunds for the years where you have over-payed your tax obligation. The IRS also has the ability to tap your bank account and even garnish wages if they see fit. Clearly, with those options at their disposal, they are less inclined to accept a small portion of what they are owed just to settle with you. Time is clearly on their side, because the longer your tax debt remains unpaid, the greater the additional interest that you will owe for your unpaid tax obligation.

The IRS has up to two years to reject or accept your offer, but it is important to note that the IRS is unlikely to accept your offer if the amount owed is significant. There may also be fees attached to using this program, which is a cost that you would not be refunded if your offer is rejected. Working with a professional can help you to navigate these IRS programs and perhaps settle any tax debt in the process.

As you can see, there is a lot that can be impacted as a result of an audit. The more complicated the requests from the IRS, the more important it is to make sure that you have professional advice to help you manage your responses to the process.

Your audit is essentially a dispute with the IRS and ignoring the communication from the IRS regarding your audit will likely only make it worse. A tax lawyer can help you to make sure that you are not missing any deadlines and it also shows the IRS that you are taking the audit seriously. Now that you understand why an audit is taking place and the importance of using professionals during the audit process, let's talk about what needs to be included when preparing for an audit of your business.

How to Prepare For Your Audit

Since you have been notified about your audit, as well as whether it will be conducted by mail or through an in-person interview, you now need to prepare for that audit. During your audit, the examiner will be checking to see if you reported all the taxable income, losses, expenses, and deductions for your business. They are also looking to make sure that all those items are in compliance with the applicable federal tax laws.

Whether you oversee your business accounting or not, it is important that you be aware of how the accounting process works so that you can answer questions being put to you. After all, just because you do not involve yourself in the day-to-day accounting does not mean that you are not responsible for what is being done in the name of your business.

Often, even if something is found to be wrong with your tax return, the worst that is likely to happen is an additional tax bill or an occasional penalty. Sometimes there are no adjustments made at all, and so the only thing that you have to pay is a day or two of inconvenience and perhaps a slightly larger bill from your accountant to cover his or her time.

Here are a few steps that you can take as part of your preparation for your audit. First, ask the IRS why your return was selected for an audit. There are a variety of reasons that may come into play including:

Specific activity on your return that does not match what you reported or high deductions related to your income, as well as filings that are inconsistent with what you reported in previous years' filings.

Automatic flags based on outlying scores found by the computer, since most businesses file electronically.

Random selection

Related examinations as mentioned previously

No matter what notification you have received from the IRS, it will contain a notice number in the upper right-hand corner. Those numbers are important because they give you additional information about the specific issues that the IRS wants you to address regarding your tax return. If you know what you are being audited for, it can help you through the preparation process, including whether you need a tax attorney or to have your CPA on hand.

Once you know what you are being audited for, you have the responsibility of gathering the related documents. There may be just a few items or a long list. It can be helpful to have all the documentation related to the tax return in question on hand, even if you are only going to give them a few pieces of requested information. If they have additional questions, then you will already have the information on hand to address it. However, it may be helpful to work through this process with a professional so you do not send more information than is necessary and possibly create a larger issue as a result.

Throughout this process, you might be thinking, while all of this knowledge is great, I want to help my business avoid triggering an audit in the first place. With that in mind, the next section is about sharing some of the common scenarios that can trigger an audit. The goal is that by avoiding these triggers, you can reduce your limited chances of being audited even further.

What Can Potentially Trigger an IRS Audit

Here are a few of the scenarios that can result in triggering an IRS audit, thus giving you tips for what to avoid whenever possible on your return. The first point has to do with your bookkeeping processes. If you delegate this task to another employee or outsource it, then it can be tempting to consider guessing at specific expenses or income at tax time. The resulting numbers are likely to be round ones, since people typically tend to use round numbers when they are estimating. The IRS is onto this fact, so if you submit a return where all the income and expenses are in multiples of $100, then you increase the likelihood of being triggered to be audited.

The reality is that even if your accounting software will round up to the nearest dollar, and the IRS is not expecting that you report your numbers down to the penny. They are going to be looking for indications that you're guessing, because that increases the likelihood that you may not be reporting all the income and expenses for your business in that year. One way to avoid this is to keep accurate records of your income and double-check your return to make sure all the income was reported on it. That will decrease the likelihood of a rounding error that could trigger a potential audit.

Another scenario that may come into play is the salaries that are being paid to corporate employees but not being reported. If your business is being taxed as a C-Corp or as a S-Corp, then you need to pay yourself a salary before the non-wage distributions are released. In a C-Corp, those non-wage distributions are taxable as dividends. With the S-Corp, those distributions are subject to ordinary income taxes, but they will not be subject to payroll taxes. If you submit your return without the entry for officer wages filled out, then you are increasing the likelihood that you are going to be put into the audit pile.

Many businesses have legitimate deductions but the problem that often triggers an audit is when those legitimate expenses are too high. For example, meals and entertainment expenses are legitimate but you need to be able to prove that the expenses are ordinary and necessary to the course of your business operations. To avoid having any problems if you are audited, then you need to make sure you keep good records. Detail the nature of the expense, and if it was a meal then put down who was there and what the purpose of the meal was.

Note that everything which you should track on the receipt, is about having details that demonstrate why the expense is a legitimate business deduction. Another way that you might be deducting meals is during business travel. These meals are deductible, but it is important to note the nature of the travel. For instance, you might be traveling to a tradeshow or seminar that is a continuing education credit for your profession. Meals during such trips can be deducted, but note the name of the trip, the dates, and where you traveled to. This helps to make sure that you are showing a legitimate connection between your business and that expense.

Remember that there is a difference between a meal related to a business meeting or business travel and the expenses for your daily lunch or favorite morning coffee. Those daily lunches and snacks that you buy for yourself are not considered legitimate tax deductions, so you need to be sure that you only report the ones that you can show are tied to a relevant business activity. While it might be common for individuals to throw those daily meals onto the business expenses, doing so can put you in the position of having an audit or having to justify those expenses to the IRS. If they find you underpaid your taxes, then you are likely going to end up paying not only the additional tax, but penalties along with it.

Do you run your business out of your home office? This is also a legitimate deduction, but the problem comes when people do not have a designated space for a home office. Instead, they might be working from their kitchen table or another space within the home that is also being used for other family activities. To be a legitimate home office, it needs to be used exclusively and regularly for your business activities. Create a legitimate workspace and then make sure that you are accurately reporting the square footage of that workspace within your home. The IRS also wants to clearly see that space is not being used by the rest of the family for other activities. Even your work computer should not be used for family activities, such as children's homework, but needs to be solely for the use of the business. Too often, people make the mistake of using the kitchen table for the office, and then thinking they can deduct the square footage for the whole kitchen. Heads up, that is not a viable deduction for a home office. Be realistic and recognize that if you try to claim a larger home office than you actually have set aside, then you might risk being pulled for an audit.

These divisions are important when it comes to an audit, because individuals can tend to overstate the square footage or usage of various items within the home as being part of the business when they do not meet the criteria for a home office. You are also able to deduct a percentage of the utility bills of the home in relation to the square footage of your home office. Being accurate on the square footage can help you to determine what portion of the bill belongs to your business.

Another point that people get tripped up on is claiming their vehicle is being used 100% for the business. That would mean the vehicle is in the business' name and is titled and registered under the business. Then the business would legitimately pay all the expenses associated with that vehicle and you would be able to claim the expenses. However, most businesses find it works better to simply claim the mileage where the car was driven to handle business related items. The standard mileage rate posted by the IRS each year is also likely to be a more attractive deduction that itemizing all the expenses related to your vehicle, including oil changes, gas, basic maintenance, tires, and more. While you might want to track those expenses to better understand what the business use is costing you in vehicle maintenance, for deduction purposes, track the mileage instead.

When you first start a new business, the reality is that you are not necessarily going to be profitable. In fact, you are more likely to see a loss the first year or two as you build a clientele, market your business, and then build your brand. Overtime, your costs will come down and your profits are going to move upwards. However, the IRS is likely to flag your return if you show repeated losses year after year. At that point, they may start to get suspicious about whether you are running a business or actually claiming deductions for a hobby under the umbrella of your business. Therefore, it is important to be sure that you are not claiming additional expenses against the business. However, if your business continues to run at a loss, you need to be prepared to prove that loss during an audit.

Now this next trigger is one that you really can't and shouldn't try to avoid. According to tax law, you are required to report all your income from all sources, so your business income needs to be reported completely and accurately, no matter whether it is high or low. Still, it is important to be aware of the fact that having a higher business income is likely to put you into the category of a greater audit risk.

There is a consistent theme with all of these potential audit triggers, which is that you need to maintain the accuracy of your records and your tax filings. While being consistently accurate is not a guarantee that you are never going to be audited, it can help to reduce your chances. However, it will also give you the peace of mind that even if you are audited your records will be accurate and stand up to any examination.

Survival Tips for Any Audit

Here are a few survival tips for any audit that you are presented with. Following them can help you to manage an audit without stressing out.

Keep good records. I have said this before, and it is still true that good recordkeeping is going to help make the audit process easier. You may decide to keep your records physically or electronically, but it is important to make sure that you are meeting all your legal requirements for your tax records. Even if the receipt is technically not required to be kept by the IRS, the reality is that you benefit by having all receipts and backup handy during any audit.

Be prepared. Since the IRS gives you the audit date well in advance, you need to make sure that you compile your records and isolate the year under consideration. If possible, downloading those records into your accounting software prior to the audit.

Be courteous to the auditor. It goes without saying that IRS auditors are not necessarily the most popular individuals but being courteous can go a long way to smooth the audit process for everyone involved. Just be sure that you do not venture into an area of niceness that could be construed as an attempt at bribery. Part of that courteousness includes dressing professionally and arriving on time or even early. Keep your conversation focused on the audit and keep your answers short and sweet.

You do have certain rights that the auditor has to respect. At the same time, when both of you are respectful to each other, the process can be completed without feelings of defensiveness or frustration. It does not mean you want to give away more information than what they are asking for, because that could mean you send them in a new direction of investigation, which is not what you want.

At the end of the day, the examiner is done and will give his conclusions. Now that you have survived your audit, let's talk about the potential outcomes of your audit and what it can mean for your business.

The Outcomes of Your Audit

No matter what the reason for your selection to be audited, the reality is that you can basically have one of three outcomes. Here are those outcomes and what they will mean for you:

The auditor or examiner will review your return and documentation, then conclude that all the information is correct. At that point, you will not owe any additional taxes and there will not be any amendments or changes to your return. This outcome is the most favorable to you and your business, although you are still going to have the costs associated with preparing for the audit, the costs of any professionals that you tap as resources during the audit, and of course, the costs of your time during the audit itself.

The auditor may find a mistake, and you may agree with their findings. If the auditor determines there are errors and you acknowledge them, then you are liable for any additional taxes that may be owed, along with the associated penalties and interest for those unpaid taxes. On the other hand, the errors might end up being in your favor and that might mean the government owes you money, although they are not going to pay you interest for the amount of money that they owe you.

The auditor finds a mistake and you disagree that it is a mistake. As a taxpayer, you do have the right to disagree with their findings, especially if they are not in your favor. You will have 30 days from the date of their findings to register your appeal. If the appeal is not favorable, you may even have the option to sue the IRS. However, it is important to consider getting professional representation if you are disputing findings to protect your rights and the rights of your business. The IRS knows they have to respect your rights, but if you do not know your rights, then it is possible that you may give away more than you intended. Having professional representation can help you to avoid potentially bringing other aspects of your business up for scrutiny by the IRS.

Tax penalties and interest can pile up during the time that you are appealing or disputing the findings of the IRS. Therefore, you may also want to count the cost of continuing the appeal process versus just paying the taxes and penalties to settle the debt and moving forward with the process of running your business. Sometimes proving that you are right to the IRS may not be worth the cost and aggravation to actually win. Recognize that the IRS has time and the law on its side, and you only have the limited resources of your business. Clearly, it is important to weigh up all the potential outcomes before you pursue a long drawn out appeal with the IRS.

Now that I have shared with you all the different aspects of being audited and how you can reduce your chances of being audited even further, it is time to talk about the most important tax deductions that you can take for your business. These are the ones that you should not miss because they can help you to reduce your tax liability. Let's get started by talking about what tax deductions mean for your business.

Chapter 4 – The Most Important Tax Deductions for Business Owners

Business owners constantly watch their cash flow to make sure that they are going to be able to cover all their overheads including their tax obligations. However, the size of your tax obligation for your business is going to depend on a variety of factors, some of which are related to the types of expenses your business incurs on a daily, weekly, and monthly basis. A few of those factors include how much your business earns in profit, how large the expenses are, and what deductions you can take.

As a business owner, you want to be sure that you are getting every break you can when it comes to your tax bill for the year. After all, if you miss one, then it could mean your bill is larger than you expected. The IRS is under no obligation to help you find out what deductions you qualify for.

Consider the fact that your business and the IRS are technically at cross purpose. After all, their goal is to collect as much tax as possible, and your goal is to reduce your tax bill and liabilities as much as possible. Still, if you are familiar with deductions and your business, then you and your tax professional should be able to find the ones that give you the most bang for your buck.

The question is how you figure out what qualifies as a legitimate deduction for your business and what doesn't qualify as a legitimate deduction. After all, if you spend time and energy collecting receipts or tracking expenses, only to find out that you cannot get the deduction, then that can become frustrating for you as a business owner. Not to mention, it can be a waste of resources that your new business might not be able to afford to part with. Those who already own a business and have been open for a while, might also find that checking deductions is a great way to find expenses that could be draining your business unnecessarily. Essentially, deductions can serve to lower your tax bill, but also help you to analyze the financial health of your business on a regular basis.

With that in mind, the goal is learning about the various tax deductions available, what they are, how you can track them, and how they can be limited by current or changing tax laws before you file your next tax return. In this chapter, I am going to focus on the different types of tax deductions available for businesses and what deductions you should not miss.

What is a Tax Deduction for a Business?

A tax deduction is an expense that you can use to reduce your taxable business profits. The difference between deductions, exemptions, and credits is that deductions, along with exemptions, are meant to reduce taxable income. Credits are meant to reduce the tax bill itself and so the combination of these two can positively impact the amount of tax that you have to pay at the end of the tax year. It is important to know what business expenses qualify to be deductions, because not every business expense is going to qualify as a tax deduction.

Since you are already tracking your business expenses, it is important to make sure that you are categorizing them correctly to be sure that your tax deductions are grouped together. Many of the available financial software options can help you with this process. Here are a few things to keep in mind as you are categorizing expenses that could be potential tax deductions.

One critical point is that there are deductions which fall above and below the line. The deductions that fall above the line lessen adjusted gross income. On the other hand, deductions below the line only lessen taxable income if the accumulation of these itemized deductions exceeds what a standard deduction is for the tax year. If you have set your business up as a partnership, a sole proprietorship, or a limited liability company, then the profit from the business is going to pass through to your individual tax return. You may find that it pushes you up into another tax bracket, which increases your tax bill. Therefore, deductions can be a way to counter that impact from the pass-through of the business profit into your tax return.

Therefore, keeping track of your deductions can help you to determine if you are going to need to itemize your deductions or if you will have to use the standard deduction instead. Some businesses may not have as many expenses as others, which can impact the number and amount of your deductions. In addition, your deductions can be subject to certain conditions, so you may find that you cannot claim all the deductions that you had originally anticipated.

Overtime, your business is going to accumulate assets and some of those assets are going to depreciate as your business ages. Therefore, you may also claim a deduction for that depreciation, although it will be limited to a specific amount each year. Next, let's talk about the various expenses that can be translated into tax deductions.

What Are Ordinary Expenses that Qualify as Tax Deductions?

Here are some of the business expenses that could be deemed tax deductions. Often, these expenses must be incurred as part of increasing or growing your business and activities that are usually part of creating profit.

The first expense we are going to discuss is the cost of goods sold. Almost all income tax systems allow for this deduction. It can be considered an expense, a reduction of gross income or a part of the calculation of your net profits. The process of determining this can be complex, so you would want to work with your accountant to determine if you can take this deduction or if you would qualify for it.

The U.S. allows a deduction for all the ordinary and necessary expenses incurred throughout the taxable year in the process of carrying out trade or business. Along the way, however, there are definitional issues that tend to come up, including the following questions:

What constitutes a trade or business? – To qualify, your business must be continuous, substantial, and have an expectation of profit.

What expenses should be considered ordinary and necessary? – Essentially, what are the expenses related to your business that help to produce income and promote your business. That means you can't expense personal items to your business, as they would not count as tax deductible.

Business deductions of the entities we discussed earlier may pass through to its members, such as in the case of a sole proprietorship. Therefore, if you are running your business and it is set up to not pay its own taxes, then you are likely going to be able to take advantage of the deductions available to your business through your personal tax return. Clearly, that can be one of the biggest benefits of a pass-through business entity for a business owner.

However, it is important that you recognize that deductions may have limits, even if they are legitimate expenses that you are trying to claim as deductions. Therefore, you may find that there is only so much that you can claim regarding your vehicles or your home office. The point is to make sure that whatever you are deducting is reported as accurately as possible in both your financials and your tax filings, annually and quarterly.

Other limitations can come into play for deducting the compensation of your key employees, lobbying, and entertainment. After all, just because you went together as a group for drinks does not mean that the business received any value from that gathering. A meeting with a potential client that ends in a sale, however, has value for the business and is more likely to be deductible. Therefore, it is important to note the purpose of any meeting that involves a meal, drinks, or entertainment. When you keep track of all the details, then you are giving yourself a better chance of arguing the deductibility of an expense, versus one that lacks those details.

You also cannot deduct any payments of fines, such as parking tickets. If your business is getting a lot of parking tickets, for instance, you might want to look deeper into your processes to help you avoid those fines. After all, those fines can be a large drain on your business, with no financial benefit. For any business owner, eliminating these types of drains is part of protecting your business financially. Looking for deductions in your expenses can also help you to take a closer look at the expenses and find ways to reduce them.

Keeping track of how money is being spent in your company will help you to determine what categories various expenses belong to. This process will also help to make it easier for you to determine what belongs in your list of deductions and what are going to be expenses that cannot be deducted and are just part of the cost of doing business.

The cost of doing business can be factored into the production of your products or services, as well as the administration that contributes to keeping your business running. After all, someone needs to pay bills, manage how employee hours are spent, and meet deadlines or compliance requirements from the government. None of that is going to contribute to your income, but without those aspects of your business, the products and services could not be provided, and your clients would not be able to purchase them. In the end, without those aspects of the business, you are not going to be able to create income.

Realistically, there are certain expenses that are considered part of the cost of doing business, so they are not going to be something that you can then deduct from your taxes. Here are a few of the items that would not qualify as a deduction:

> Cost of products, including charges related to freight or shipping
>
> Cost of storing your business' products
>
> Your direct labor costs related to producing your products
>
> Overhead expenses for a factory or warehouse

If you have questions regarding your specific business expenses and which ones are going to qualify as deductions, then you need to talk with your tax professional to determine what qualifies and what does not. Now I am going to discuss what capitalized items are and how depreciation works in your business.

What Are Capitalized Items and Depreciation?

As a business grows, you are likely going to continue to purchase items that are necessary for your business to function. In manufacturing, for instance, you are going to purchase equipment that helps you to produce the different products that you sell. If you are providing services, then you might need specific tools to provide those services. These items are going to provide benefits to your business in the years after you purchase them, so these items are going to need to be capitalized.

Examples of capitalization include plant and equipment or the fees that relate to the development of assets, such as patents. The result of capitalization means that you may be able to receive a tax deduction for cost recovery over the next few years. What happens is that your business is allowed to deduct a portion of its cost ratably over several tax years. Depreciation is the term used for the deductions taken for tangible assets and amortization is the term used for the costs associated with intangible assets.

Both of these terms are used to represent the accounting methods that allocate the cost of assets over their useful life, but also helps you to account for the value decline of an item over its lifetime. For the purposes of your tax filings, your business can deduct the cost of tangible assets purchased as a business expense. However, you need to follow the depreciation rules that are outlined by the IRS.

When it comes to understanding depreciation, you have to recognize that it does not represent cash flow. Instead, it is a tool that businesses can use to allow for the write-off of an asset's value over time. For example, if your business were to purchase equipment that costs $50,000 then you can write off the entire cost during the first year or opt to write off the value of the asset over the 10-year life period of the piece of equipment. What makes it an appealing option is that you have the benefit of the deduction over ten years, instead of taking it all at once. Why would a business owner want to take a deduction over multiple years?

It can help them to offset tax liabilities in the coming years, especially as the business' income increases with the growth of the business. Companies also use depreciation to express the loss of market value throughout the life of an asset. There are a few assets that can lose value, such as currency and real estate. During the 2008 housing crisis, there were homeowners who saw a loss in the value of their homes by up to 60%. Clearly, as a business, it can be a tricky thing to balance the various losses and reductions in value that happen throughout the life of your business.

As you can see, there are benefits to having the ability to deduct these large expenses, which can balance the fact that you need to invest capital into your business. You might want to consider the type of investments that you make in your business based on when some of these new tax deductions and limits end or take effect. In chapter five, there is a section related to bonus depreciation according to the Tax Cuts and Jobs Act changes. Read about that bonus depreciation as you plan for capital investments, as the timing could impact the size of the deduction that you can take.

Now let's talk about a few of the common deductions that are beneficial to business owners.

Top Tax Deductions for Businesses

Deductions found in business expenses are meant to help with the costs of running your business. As a business owner, you know that most expenditures have the possibility of being deducted, even if there are limits and timing issues that relate to those deductions.

To take advantage of all the deductions that you qualify for and that benefit your business, you need to have a quality recordkeeping system. Technology can provide you with a variety of options to allow you to transfer receipts into an electronic format. This is the type of format which can make it easier to keep your records for a longer period of time in a way that will keep them from deteriorating the way physical records can.

Here are a few of those deductions that are claimed by businesses on their Schedule C. You can look through these and even discuss taking advantage of them with your tax professional if they apply to your business or industry.

1. Car and truck expenses – It is a rare business that does not use a vehicle in some way or another. These vehicles could be a car, truck, or van. You can deduct all the expenses related to the care and maintenance of the vehicle. However, you also have the option to track the mileage and simply take the deduction for that instead.

2. Contract labor – As a small or new business, you might have opted to use freelancers or contractors to complete work or meet your labor needs. The costs of that labor are deductible. You just need to issue a 1099-MISC to any contractors that you paid over $600 to in that tax year.

3. Supplies – The cost of all the items that you use in your business, such as cleaning supplies or postage, are all fully deductible expenses. They are treated as non-incidental materials and supplies that are not going to depreciate. To take advantage of this deduction, it is important that you keep all your receipts related to these items.

4. Rent on your business property. The cost of renting a space for your business is fully deductible, regardless of whether it is an office, boutique, or other type of facility. For those who may be renting a manufacturing factory or other space, then you need to be sure to keep track of all your rental expenses to determine what you can deduct.

5. Taxes – Hard to believe, but the fees for licenses, regulatory fees, and the taxes on real estate, plus your employer taxes, are all fully deductible. Self-employed individuals cannot deduct half of their self-employment tax because it is not considered deductible.

6. Insurance – The cost of the insurance for your business, including malpractice coverage, flood insurance, and business continuation insurance. Health care insurance may be deductible but check with your tax professional to determine what is deductible and how much of your costs qualify. Individuals may be able to deduct their premiums and if you choose to pay premiums for your employees, your business may be able to deduct those as well.

These are just a few of the deductions available to your business. Working with your tax professional, you can find more deductions that are specific to your business. The point of this chapter is recognizing that there are a variety of deductions available to businesses and corporations. You need to be proactive in looking for the deductions that your business may qualify for and then making sure that you have all the appropriate documentation to back you up in taking that deduction.

Today there are a variety of software options that can help you to keep your receipts organized. For instance, you can scan your receipts and include specific information regarding the business event. It can give you the ability to classify them according to the approved IRS categories. The benefit of using this type of software is that you can then keep your records electronically. That allows you to back them up and can protect your company if you are ever in a position of being audited by the IRS.

Physical copies of paperwork can be damaged or destroyed, which could then make it difficult for you to defend your deductions in the future. As technology continues to advance, your options to protect your business financials continue to grow. To benefit your company, you need to be open to exploring these options. Along with that, there are also going to be changes to deductions as tax laws are updated or changed.

There may have been tax deductions that were available in the past that with changing tax laws may no longer apply. Other new deductions have been added to the tax laws, so you may have new deductions that you qualify for instead. With that in mind, let's talk about some of the changes that took place in 2018 due to the Tax Cuts and Jobs Act.

Chapter 5 – The Impact of the Tax Cuts and Job Act on Your Business

Over the past two years, there have been a variety of legislative changes in the United States that have impacted businesses. The current administration is focused on reducing the number of regulations that impact small and medium-sized businesses, as well as updating the tax code to reduce the amount of tax being paid by businesses. The goal of these changes was to allow businesses to reinvest the savings which come from not having to implement various regulations and from tax reductions, into equipment and jobs.

While there are experts that could argue the Tax Cuts and Job Act was a step in the right direction, there are just as many that might argue this legislative move would not benefit the business community. Regardless of your opinion of this act as a business owner, the reality is that it will impact your business and the amount of tax that you will be paying. Additionally, there are forms that will be changing, so it is important to make sure that you have the latest forms when collecting information from your employees.

The wording throughout this chapter can be a bit more complicated, so if you have any questions about how these changes are going to impact your business specifically, it is important to make sure that you check in with your tax professional. They can sit down with you and work through the aspects of the law that apply to you and your business.

Throughout this chapter, I am going to cover the Tax Cuts and Job Act, giving you insight into how it will impact your business and how you file your taxes, especially if you have chosen one of the entities that allows you to pass income through from your business to your personal tax return. Let's get started!

Corporate Tax Changes

The Tax Cuts and Jobs Act has made a significant number of changes to the corporate income tax and taxes for pass-through businesses. Most of these changes to the corporate tax code are going to be permanent, meaning they will not have an expiration date. The law changed the corporate income tax rate, making it 21% from the 35% it was previously. It also eliminated the corporate alternative minimum tax.

Corporate businesses can now deduct the full cost of qualified new investments the year those investments are made for the next five years. Bonus deprecation phases down in 20%-point increments starting in 2023, but it will be fully eliminated after 2026. That means you can enjoy an 80%-point depreciation in 2023, but a 60%-point depreciation in 2024. This can benefit companies that are looking to make significant capital investments for future growth. However, there are also some businesses that will not be eligible for this bonus depreciation. These businesses include real estate companies that deduct 100% of their business interest or a dealership with floor-plan financing and annual gross receipts of more than $25 million during the past three tax years.

Other deductions are going to be limited, such as the amount of net business interest and net operating losses. The domestic production activities deduction has been eliminated and there are modified smaller provisions throughout the tax code. If your business is involved in research and experimentation, then you are going to be able to amortize those expenses over five years starting in 2022.

Depending on how you have set up your business, you are also going to have to deal with the changes related to your pass-through income deductions. It is a complex change that involves being able to deduct 20% of your qualified business income if your taxable income for joint filers is under $315,000. Now if your taxable income exceeds this amount, your deduction may be reduced depending on the type of business that you run, and the wages paid. However, once your taxable income reaches $415,000 for joint filers, then the QBI is going to be zero, meaning you no longer have a deduction. Your losses are also going to be limited. Working with your tax professional, you can determine how that will impact your deductions in the coming years.

If you do business internationally or own a portion of an international company, your business may also have reduced or no taxes due on the money earned from these businesses. To determine what you may or may not owe, it is important to check with your tax professional.

Many of these changes can sound complicated and the wording can make it difficult to determine what applies to your business and what does not. Therefore, you need to recognize that you and your employee who handles payroll will have to be trained to make sure that all withholdings and deductions are being handled properly.

Your tax professional is also going to be key to this process, especially as you start looking at your deductions for the upcoming tax year. Before we start talking about the need to sit down with your tax professional or accountant, let's talk about a few of the changes that are going to impact your payroll processes.

Talking About Payroll Changes

While the primary focus of this law was reducing taxes, it was also meant to address forms that had been virtually the same for decades. The idea is that by updating the W-4 form, employees can have their withholding more accurately match their tax bill, thus leaving more of their paycheck in their pockets. The idea is that there will be fewer tax refunds as a result, but that employees would prefer bigger paychecks throughout the year instead of one big payout once a year.

One of the changes that is a result of the Tax Cuts and Job Act is that the W-4 form, typically completed by new employees prior to receiving their first paycheck, has been updated. There are a few key changes that were made, although the new form has not been officially released for use. The changes include the calculations page being updated to reflect changed amounts in B, F, and G. The worksheet Tables 1 and 2 were also updated to reflect the new federal income tax withholding schedules. This will make it easier for employees to make sure they are withholding the right amount to avoid owing when they file their taxes next year.

The W-4 can be updated at any time by your employees, so be sure that once the official federal updated W-4 is released, they have the opportunity to update their information accordingly. You also want to have the updated W-4 as part of your onboarding package for any new employees. Depending on the state, they may also be opting to update their W-4, so be sure to check with your state to make sure you have their latest version of the W-4. It is important that you keep your forms up to date, as they will help you to navigate the withholding going forward with the new tax law.

Another change related to payroll taxes that is different in 2019 relates to the Social Security withholding. In 2019, the Social Security Administration (SSA) announced that there would be an increase to the maximum withholding, which is the maximum amount that can be taken from an employee's income to pay into the Social Security fund. This maximum withholding is typically determined every year based on a formula from the government. In 2019, that amount is $8,239.80, which is $132,900 x 6.2%, but it is important to remember that amount can change from year to year. It has steadily increased over the last decade and is likely to continue to do so as the demands on the Social Security fund continue to increase.

As an employer, there is no maximum Social Security tax payable, simply because as your business grows, you are likely to add employees. Thus, your share of this tax is going to increase as well. Still, the overall focus of these changes is to make it appealing to add employees and invest in your business. With that in mind, let's talk about a few changes meant to appeal to companies looking to add benefits for their employees. Along the way, we will also talk about other changes that can impact your corporation.

Additional Benefits for Companies Creating Change

Companies that are offer their employees paid family and medical leave are now going to be able to take advantage of a new tax credit. It applies to wages paid in the tax years that start in December 2017 and end before January 2020. While it is limited in time frame, businesses can benefit from adding this benefit because it will be a draw for potential employees.

The credit will be determined by a percentage of the wages paid out to those qualifying employees that are on leave for up to 12 weeks during the tax year. That percentage ranges from 12.5% to 25%, so it can provide an incentive for those companies on the fence about providing these types of leave for their employees. What makes these types of leave appealing is that they allow employees to take time off to care for family or to expand their family without losing their position at work. Having it be paid time off means that they will be able to take the full allotted leave period without the potential financial crunch that comes with an unpaid leave.

As you can see, there are a variety of changes that can positively impact the course of your business, but there are also changes that clearly define what types of accounting methods your business can use. For instance, small business taxpayers with gross receipts annually of $25 million or less are going to be able to continue using the cash method of accounting. To qualify, they need to meet the income limit for the past three years.

There are also changes to the conversion from an S-Corp to the C-Corp. Under the prior law, this conversion resulted in net adjustments to prevent amounts from being duplicated or omitted as a result of the change to your accounting method. Now the period for including those net adjustments has been changed to six years and it applies to those net adjustments that will decrease your taxable income and ones that increase your taxable income as well. If your taxable income goes up, then that can mean your tax liability could be increasing as a result of these changes.

Some businesses have enjoyed the benefits of the prior law that allowed for all interest paid to be fully deductible. Now the deductible interest amount has been capped to 30% of your adjusted taxable income. It can be a factor that helps to reduce your tax bill for the current tax year. Many individuals have been surprised to find that their tax bill has gone up with the new tax law. If you find that is the case with your business, then it is important to consider working with your tax professional to make sure that you have captured all the deductions that apply to your business.

Other Business-Related Changes

Here are a few other changes that relate to the new tax law which could impact your business. Many of these changes may not impact your business, depending on its size or industry. To make sure that you are not taking deductions that no longer apply, you need to go over what deductions still apply to your business and what you might qualify for as the owner or manager of your business entity. As you read through these deductions, please keep in mind that some may not have applied to your business in the past and may not apply in the future. However, there may be deductions that you could now qualify for or that may now impact your business.

Ultimately, the focus of all these changes is to improve the tax landscape for businesses, particularly corporations, with the goal of having them bring the key operations of their business back into the United States. This goal is particularly targeting multi-national corporations who may not have seen the United States as particularly friendly in their tax laws during the past few administrations.

It is also important to note that there are a variety of changes in the new tax law specifically meant to target those taxpayers and businesses who are conducting business outside of the United States. These changes are meant to encourage multi-national companies to bring more of their operations back into the United States, with the hope that it will create more jobs in various sectors for those living in the U.S.

Other changes include the Section 199 deduction, which is being eliminated for C-Corp taxpayers after December 31, 2018. This deduction was often known as the domestic production activities deduction or the manufacturers' deduction. For those who did not have a business in the manufacturing sector, this change may not have a large impact. However, manufacturing businesses will have to be sure that they do not try to take this deduction moving forward.

Compensation deductions for the funds paid to the main or principal executive officers typically cannot exceed $1 million annually, although this is subject to a transition rule for anything that might be paid due to binding contracts put into effect before November 2, 2017. Note that this means all new binding contracts are going to be subject to these limits. While that might not impact your small or medium business, if your corporation is larger and negotiates higher compensation packages for their executives, then these changes could impact how those packages are assessed in the future.

Another important point to keep in mind is that net operating losses (NOLs) are going to be capped at around 80% and you will not be able to offset or carry back NOLs to previous tax years going forward. With that in mind, non-corporate taxpayers are also finding that their ability to deduct excess business losses is going to be affected. However, if a loss is disallowed in one tax year, it may be able to be carried forward into the next tax year and then deducted as a NOL. Only the individual taxpayer is going to benefit from this, especially if the business has already exceeded its applicable threshold. Working with your tax professional or accountant, you can determine how this will impact your business and your potential tax liability.

Another point to keep in mind is that deductions for cafeteria or other food options on the premises of the employer will be non-deductible after 2025. Meal expenses that are incurred during any business travel are still considered 50% deductible. Previously, the meals provided to an employee on their premises were 100% deductible by the employer, along with other employer-provided fringe benefits. Today, there have been many changes that impact the deductibility of these types of benefits. As an employer, you may want to reexamine whether these benefits are still worth the investment.

As an employer, you might have included a transportation benefit for your employees, one that may have including commuting transportation. While you might have been able to deduct that in the past, the reality is that now you are not going to be able to deduct those expenses. The only exception appears to be if the transportation is related to the safety of the employee. Employers cannot even deduct the cost of transportation fringe benefits, such as parking allowances, public transportation passes, or even a car or van pooling. Still, these benefits remain tax-free to your employees if you do offer them.

When it comes to planning for your tax liability and taking advantage of the deductions available, you should sit down with your tax professional and discuss what your business now qualifies for and what changes apply specifically to your business. You may find that there are new options that you qualify for in order to reduce your tax liability over the next few years. It is also important to note that some of these changes are not permanent. Therefore, you also need to discuss with your tax professional what the impact of pursuing some of these changes or deductions are, knowing that the credits or deductions making them appealing right now will not be available in the future.

Ultimately, these are decisions that you are going to make based on what is best for your business, while balancing the impact of your business decisions on your tax liability. As the owner, your business priorities are going to play a part in the choices that you make and what you choose to pursue in terms of change. Not everyone is going to choose the same path, but that is what makes owning a business so unique to you and your ownership style.

Many business owners must also count the costs related to being compliant with the new tax law and be prepared to expend the time and resources needed accordingly. There will also be decisions regarding whether you want to continue in an area that may require a significant amount of capital to do what is necessary to remain compliant.

You will have to make sure that you are using the right forms and that you have trained your employees who work on your payroll to implement the new changes. After all, making mistakes could impact your tax liability and potentially result in penalties or fines.

Throughout this chapter, the focus has been on sharing some of the changes that have occurred due to the new tax law. However, this is not a comprehensive list. You will need to do research that is specific to your industry or business type to determine if there are additional areas where you need to make changes in order to remain compliant.

Not every business is going to find that they need to make dramatic changes, but that does not mean you can just ignore the new deductions or alterations to the tax law, hoping it doesn't apply to you. Doing your research and connecting with professionals can help you to make sure that you are not missing key information necessary for the filing of your tax return or that impacts your withholdings.

At this point, you now have a guide that can help you to navigate tax information related to your business entity, payroll taxes, deductions, audits, and more. Working through this book, you are going to have the knowledge to make the right choices for your business. You will be setting the right foundation for the future of your business and those who work with you to help you fulfill the mission and the goals that you have defined for your company.

Conclusion

Throughout this book, the focus has been on sharing what type of business entities are available and the various tax implications that are the result of registering your business legally. In Chapter one, I shared all the different types of entities and how they differ from each other. That process also involved exploring what advantages each entity had to offer but also what disadvantages were related to specific entities.

Depending on your business, the disadvantages of one entity may actually prove to be advantages. Reviewing this information can help you to make a wise decision to meet the needs of your business now and into the future. However, once you have decided on the entity that works for your business, then you need to start figuring out the various tax scenarios that could impact your business.

One of those scenarios is the taxes related to handling the payroll, which I discussed in chapter two. When you think about the addition of employees, there are a lot of dates and regulations that you have to follow in order to keep your business compliant. If your tax payments are not made promptly, then you are going to risk penalties, fines, and perhaps even an audit of your payroll by the state.

Speaking of audits, chapter three focused on what is involved in an audit, how they are conducted, what are potential triggers for an audit, and then managing the process to complete the audit successfully. Keep in mind that audits are not the end of the world and many are completed with little cost to the business that is audited. However, even if the audit ends up costing you a significant amount of cash, you can still survive the process. In fact, your business can thrive after an audit. Working with professionals can help you to navigate the audit process successfully.

Chapters four and five are focused on tax deductions and the impact of recent changes to the tax laws through the Tax Cuts and Jobs Act. This guide can give you a place to start in determining what changes will impact your business and what will not play a part in your business going forward. It can also be a place to access information on if there

SMALL BUSINESS TAXES & ACCOUNTING GUIDE

are new deductions that you might be able to benefit from. Reviewing this chapter can be a great starting point to inform your discussion with your tax professional or accountant.

May the start of your business be guided by the information included in these chapters, and may it help you to determine the best options to grow your company going forward. The reality is that every business is going to make choices that are best for their growth. However, it is important to also understand that there are tax implications that can go along with those choices.

An employer might offer specific benefits to their employees, even if the deduction is no longer available, because of the impact that those benefits have on the overall culture and working environment of the business. As the owner of your business, it is up to you to determine what is right for you as the owner, for your employees, and for the overall health of your business.

BONUS - Quickbook Guide

Chapter 1 – What is QuickBooks?....................................71

Targeted for Small and Medium Businesses.......................................71

Chapter 2 – No Matter Your Business, QuickBooks Can Help......76

QuickBooks Self-Employed...77

QuickBooks Simple Start..77

QuickBooks Simple Start, Essentials, and Plus..................................78

QuickBooks Pro Edition..78

QuickBooks Premier Edition...79

QuickBooks Enterprise Solutions...79

Chapter 3 – Basics for Navigating QuickBooks...........................81

Adding and Searching for Data...81

Understanding the Financial Health of Your Business........................82

Tools for Determining Your Financial Health......................................83

Chapter 4 – Understanding Your Tax Liability............................87

Tracking Business Expenses to Determine Deductions......................87

Estimating Tax Payments with QuickBooks..88

Chapter 5 – Options for Payroll and Timekeeping......................92

Payroll Through QuickBooks Online..92

QuickBooks Payroll Services for Desktop Versions............................93

What Is Offered in the Payroll Service?..94

Time Keeping and Tracking Labor Costs..97

Chapter 6 – Deciding What is Right for You.................................99

Use QuickBooks to Apply for Financing...100

Determining What Is Right For Your Business....................................101

Chapter 1 – What is QuickBooks?

No matter the type of business you own or if you are self-employed, keeping track of your financials is part of the administration of your business. It is not only critical in helping you understand what it costs to run your business and whether it is profitable, your financials are key to understanding what your tax liability is.

There are so many nuggets of information about the health of your business that can be gleaned from your financials. You need to understand how much it costs you to provide your product or service, your overhead costs associated with the administration of your business, and if you are selling your product or services at a profit or a loss.

Many business owners can find handling their financials to be a complicated process, one that leaves them feeling frustrated and lacking the critical information necessary to make decisions for their business.

While you can hire an accountant, for many small businesses, hiring an accountant or accounting service can be cost prohibitive. However, in today's high-tech world, there are software alternatives that can provide the benefits of an accounting service for a budget-friendly price.

QuickBooks is just such a program. Geared toward business owners and those that are self-employed, QuickBooks is a web-based program that allows you to input all the aspects of your business finances and to generate reports, such as your profit and loss statement. You can break down your financials by quarters or by specific time periods throughout the year so that you can to do a deeper analysis of the growth or lack of growth in your business.

Targeted for Small and Medium Businesses

QuickBooks is an accounting software program targeted at small businesses. The software can track both your sales and expenses, as well as record your daily transactions. Another useful benefit is that it can be used to generate and track invoices. Cash flow is the lifeblood of any small business. Thus, it is critical to know what invoices are outstanding and what has been paid. With QuickBooks, a business owner is quickly able to determine which customers are overdue on their invoices and take the necessary steps to ensure payment.

For business owners, it is also key to track the money that you owe to vendors, tax agencies, your landlord, utilities, and more. Using an accounting software system, you can input your expenses and then schedule the payments. Again, it is about managing the cash flow of your business and understanding what money is coming in and what is going out.

Of course, no accounting software is complete without reports for planning, tax filing, and more. You can use it to generate month- and year-end reports that can help you to prepare for your quarterly and annual business taxes. What makes this accounting software so attractive is that it can be managed by a business owner or outsourced to a book-keeper. Working with this software is meant to be intuitive and user-friendly. Here are the top eight uses associated with QuickBooks:

1. Manage Your Sales and Income

You can use the software to track sales by customer. By reviewing your Accounts Receivable Aging Report (ARAR), you have access to the details regarding current and past due invoices. This report also helps you to manage aging invoices, allowing you to target the invoices that have reached 30, 60, or 90 days past due.

QuickBooks also offers you a convenient method to allow your customers to pay electronically, allowing you to take payment via credit cards or bank accounts using an ACH payment. With online payment options, your customers can find it easier to pay their invoices and that means you get access to your cash faster.

Additionally, as an owner, you can analyze when your sales are at a peak and then use that data to help you make changes during the slower periods. It can also help you to determine which customers are slower paying and help you to adjust your expenses accordingly to manage your cash flow effectively.

2. Automatic Way to Track Expenses

QuickBooks can be connected to your business bank account and your business credit cards. All your expenses are then automatically pulled into the software and categorized. If you have a cash or check transaction, you can easily record it to keep your records up to date. This accounting software can be a great tool to keep you on-time paying your bills as well.

One of the ways that you can do this is by creating an Accounts Payable Report that will let you know what bills are due and what is past due. As a business owner, it can help you to better understand what potential issues you have and help you to better manage your cash flow.

3. Gain Insights into Your Business

Reports available through QuickBooks can give you insights into the growth or lack of growth in your business. Plus, if you are looking to find an investor to access capital for equipment or expansion efforts, then these reports can help you to showcase how well your business is doing. Available reports include profit and loss, balance sheet, and statement of cash flows.

4. Managing Your Payroll

To keep your business growing, you may have already expanded and added employees. With the ongoing changes to tax laws, it can be a complicated process to make sure that you are withdrawing the right amount for taxes. With a QuickBooks payroll subscription, you can access the latest payroll tax tables, making it easier to calculate what your employer payroll tax responsibilities are and how much is the responsibility of your employee.

With technology today, the idea of traditional paychecks has been replaced with direct deposit into your employees' bank account. When you use QuickBooks payroll, you can offer direct deposit, as well as automatically calculate federal and state payroll taxes. The program will also complete the various tax forms for you, while providing you the ability to electronically pay your taxes, both federal and state. For business owners, this option gives you an electronic trail to follow if there are any questions regarding your tax payments.

5. What Have You Got?

Your inventory is a huge capital investment, so it is critical that you can track it. Not only do you need to know what you have and what is on order, you also need to understand what it costs and what your margins are for those products. While you might be able to track all of that information using Excel or another type of spreadsheet, it can become time-consuming. One wrong entry can send your whole system off course. QuickBooks offers reports to help you track inventory, so you can have a list of your inventory, what is on hand, the average cost of an item, and what the total value of your inventory is.

As a business owner, you may be unknowingly tying up large amounts of capital in inventory that is not selling. Having a quality inventory system in place will allow you to make decisions regarding your inventory. These include reducing your purchasing of some items and increasing the purchasing of others to drive your sales upward, while controlling your costs.

You also have the added benefit of using these reports to find the highest sale items, helping you to pare down your offerings based on what is selling well and what is not.

6. Reduce Your Tax Season Stress

Tax season can be a stressful time for a business owner. Not only do you have to mail out W-2s and 1099s, you have to file the taxes for the business at both the state and federal levels. If you go to your tax professional with a box of receipts for your business, that is going to cost you in two ways. First, it will cost you in terms of how much you are charged by your tax professional. Secondly, it could cost you in potential deductions because a receipt might be missing.

QuickBooks allows you give your tax professional access to your data, giving them the information that they need and minimizing the amount of time they need to spend searching through bank statements and receipts. Plus, you can increase the accuracy of your tax return because all the income and expenses are accounted for in QuickBooks. With a feature to scan receipts, you can keep an electronic copy, instead of trying to hold onto paper receipts throughout the year.

As you can see, there are a variety of benefits that come with using the accounting software provided by QuickBooks, either through its web-based functions or by purchasing the software outright. Throughout this guide, we are going to cover the basics of QuickBooks, giving you an understanding of the various options and functions available to help you in using this software to the fullest for your business.

Let's get started!

Chapter 2 – No Matter Your Business, QuickBooks Can Help

One of the best parts of QuickBooks is that it is not a cookie-cutter, one-size-fits-all type of accounting software. Instead, QuickBooks offers a variety of options to fit the needs of your business. Each of their options provides the tools for routine and accurate accounting. Plus, you can eliminate having multiple software options to manage your financials because everything can be done through one application.

If you want to use QuickBooks online, there are five different versions to choose from. These options come with a monthly subscription fee, although QuickBooks does offer discounts for businesses that opt to pay for a year or more in advance. Depending on the cash flow of your business, it might be easier to have a smaller monthly payment, but again, this can be changed to fit the needs of your business and your budget.

QuickBooks online versions provide a wide level of compatibility. No matter your platform, the online version will work because the software is not running on your desktop or laptop. This option also provides an additional level of security and protection from data loss, plus you always have access to the updated software version. With no information being kept on your server or desk top, you can access your information even if your hardware dies unexpectedly.

As your business grows, you may want to consider moving to a desktop version, which QuickBooks also offers. This option has a variety of features that can be key to tracking the growth of your company and understanding its financial position. You can opt for an annual subscription for your desktop version, which allows you to access add-on services and the latest security updates.

However, as your software ages, QuickBooks does discontinue different features, which means that you will have to upgrade your product to continue enjoying the benefits of add-ons and security features. For instance, in 2019, QuickBooks began to discontinue add-ons and security updates for the QuickBooks Desktop 2016 versions. The fully supported products include Desktop Pro and Premier for 2019, 2018, and 2017, as well as others from 2017 forward.

What is the difference between the 2019 versions and the 2016 versions? According to QuickBooks, there are productivity boosting features, meant to assist in saving time and keeping you organized. There are also system requirements to be considered, so it is important to determine if your current hardware can support an upgrade.

Part of the process of upgrading includes converting your company file of data so it will work with your new version of QuickBooks. As part of the process, QuickBooks will prompt you to create a backup and will verify the integrity of your data. Thus, if there are any issues during the upgrade process, your data will remain secure.

Here is a little bit of information about each of the online and desktop versions, which can help you to determine what will work for your business and the options available for your business as it grows.

QuickBooks Self-Employed

This online version of QuickBooks comes with the fewest features and the lowest monthly cost. You can manage your income and expenses, create invoices and accept payments for those invoices. There are also various reports to help you understand your business outcomes. Additionally, it includes the function to estimate your quarterly taxes. You can record when those are paid within the software as well.

QuickBooks Simple Start

This version is also online and geared toward small businesses and sole proprietors. It has the added benefit of being easy to upgrade as your business grows. It has everything that you find in the self-employed version, plus it provides the ability to track sales taxes, maximize your tax deductions, and send estimates to your customers.

For a business that is starting to grow beyond the simple functions of tracking expenses and invoices, Simple Start can be a great way to dip your business toe into the water without a large expense.

QuickBooks Simple Start, Essentials, and Plus

This online version allows you to create estimates, invoices, track sales, payments, and inventory, along with all the features found in the Simple Start version. It can also give you the ability to share data with your accountant at tax time. If you want to add the payroll function, then you can do that as well. With over 100 customizable reports, you can find out everything you need to know about the financials of your business to keep it running smoothly and to target areas of growth.

Another benefit is that because this version is online, you can send invoices, reports, and estimates right from the software. Meaning that you don't have to go from one application to another, thus streamlining your invoicing and reporting.

Finally, this online version allows you to add options that work for your business, making it a truly customizable software package. If you want to add budgeting, the ability to 1099 contractors, and sales tools, these options are available. Therefore, you can customize the accounting software to fit the needs of your company now and into the future.

Each option comes with a 30-day trial, allowing you to test-drive the software and find the right options for your business. The cost of your subscription will depend on what you choose to include. The nice part about their subscription base is that as your business grows, you can upgrade your QuickBooks and integrate your data that is already on their platform.

However, for medium sized businesses, the ideal QuickBooks option might be a desktop version. Read on to learn about the options available with the desktop software.

QuickBooks Pro Edition

While this version offers much of the functionality of the online versions, it can also be integrated with other software packages, such as Microsoft Outlook and Excel. You can also have it loaded onto a server and three users can be working in the software at the same time. However, if it is not loaded on a server, then that option will not be available. For a business that is starting to grow, having the ability to allow your sales staff to create sales invoice can be a powerful tool and one that QuickBooks offers through this multiple user feature.

If you plan on licensing this software and using it for three years, then you will pay a flat fee. Keep in mind, that does not include annual up-grades, phone support, or data backups. These features would all come at additional costs. On the other hand, a subscription service would give you the access to annual upgrades, phone support, and data backups as part of your annual subscription pricing.

QuickBooks Premier Edition

As you grow your business, you can also grow your QuickBooks ac-counting service software. The Premier Edition, which is offered as a desktop version, provides industry-specific reporting, business planning tools and forecasting for sales and expenses.

When you are analyzing your business and where it is headed, you need the ability to track your sales and back orders. The hope is that you are busy enough that you will have multiple sales orders, so know-ing what is fulfilled, what needs to be fulfilled, and what is in process is key to your success. Tracking your costs can be the difference be-tween being profitable and struggling to keep the doors open.

By using an accounting software that offers you the ability to track the costs associated with finished products and your inventory, you can ac-curately reflect your costs in your pricing models and adjust as needed.

QuickBooks Enterprise Solutions

For medium-sized businesses, this desktop edition could be the one for you. It is the most powerful version of the software, designed to handle the demands of a medium or large business, especially if you are ex-panding and will have multiple locations. One of the aspects that makes this effective for multiple locations is that you can have up to 30 simultaneous users at any given time.

Plus, this version encompasses all the features of the smaller editions and gives you a few large-scale features. These large-scale features include tracking of up to 100,000 inventory items, as well as being able to manage fixed assets and employees. For those who are looking for the right server to store this QuickBooks version, it is compatible with Linux servers.

Training your staff to use the software is simple as well, because QuickBooks offers tutorials that walk you through the functions step-by-step. Having these aspects can give you the tools to grow your business and monitor your progress. These tutorials are also helpful for learning the software yourself or answering questions that you may have as your business gets more complex and you want to include additional features.

Depending on the type of business you run and its size, there are going to be aspects of QuickBooks that you may need sooner than others. However, the beauty of this accounting software is that as your business develops, you can maintain consistency in terms of the accounting software used.

Now that you have an idea of the versions available through Quick-Books, it is time to talk about navigating QuickBooks and some of the common features to be found across all the available versions.

Chapter 3 – Basics for Navigating QuickBooks

When it comes to running a business, having critical financial information at your fingertips can be important when making business decisions. QuickBooks provides that critical information about your business right on its dashboard when you first log into the program, regardless of the version. This information includes the profit and loss of your business, your expenses, a list of your bank accounts, invoices outstanding, and your sales summary.

The dashboard is a powerful tool and a jumping off point for navigating through QuickBooks to any area of the software. Your data is organized in such a way that you can easily find what you need. However, the benefit of QuickBooks is that you can easily navigate away from the main dashboard into the areas necessary for the every day accounting needs of your business.

Let's start by focusing on adding and find key pieces of information, such as invoices or expenses.

Adding and Searching for Data

If there is information that you need to add to a specific category, then you can do it right from the plus menu at the top of your dashboard. You can do just about anything from this menu, including creating invoices, noting the receipt of a payment, or add an expense. Doing so will update your dashboard to reflect this new information, thus giving you the most up-to-date snapshot of your business' finances.

Once you have created a variety of invoices and checks within your software, then you might need to locate one to address a question or make an adjustment. Using the click search at the top, you can enter the check number, date, or amount and the system will search and find the best matches to your search terms.

There is also the left-hand navigation bar. Under this navigation bar, you can find main categories, such as banking, invoicing, expenses, employees, reports, and more. Once you click on one of these categories, such as invoicing, you can find additional options. Under invoicing, for instance, there are categories for invoices, customers, all sales, as well as products and services.

Under each of those smaller categories, you can add information about your customers, sales, and products or services. Not only will you have all the information recorded to understand where your business stands financially, you can also focus on customers or sales trends through the reports feature.

Another great icon for navigating is the gear icon, which allows you to look at specific tools for your business. This menu gives you access to your company's QuickBooks account, your custom form styles, recurring transactions, and even the ability to import data from another QuickBooks version or from another accounting software. There are also some advanced tools, including reconciling, budgeting, and your audit log.

Using each of these options is fairly simple, which makes QuickBooks an appealing option for those business owners looking for accounting software but that are not in a position to afford a full-time accounting staff or an accountant.

Understanding the Financial Health of Your Business

There are a variety of tools within the QuickBooks software that can assist you in determining how well your business is doing financially. One of the first tools are your financial statements, which can also be referred to as financial reports. These are detailed records of a business' financial activities. These are critical components to understanding if your business is making or losing money.

Your financial statements include the following:

- Balance sheet – Provides a snapshot of what is owned, what is owed, and what your business is worth. You can spot the strengths and weaknesses of your business, allowing you to make critical investment decisions to help your business grow.

- Income statement (which can also be referred to as the profit and loss statement) – Allows you to see your total income, gross profit, expenses, and net income or net loss. Use it to evaluate where you can increase income and reduce expenses. You can also click on a specific number for a more detailed transaction list. QuickBooks can also calculate your expenses as a percentage of income to determine where you might be overspending or underspending, depending on the category.

- Cash flow statement – Evaluate whether there is enough cash coming in to pay the expenses associated with your business. You can get a clear view of your cash flow over a defined time period. You can determine where your money comes from and where it is being spent.

The nice thing about QuickBooks is that you do not have to wait till the end of a quarter to find out how your business is doing. That information is available in real time, allowing you to generate and review your financial statements anytime. Having this information can help you to make decisions that can positively impact your business, such as identifying areas where you are losing money and then adjusting accordingly.

As a business owner, you can also identify specific areas of your business that could benefit from a capital investment and how that can impact your growth or set you up to take advantage of future opportunities.

You can also generate your financial statements and then send them via email to others, including a potential lender or investor.

Now that you know a little bit about the usefulness of financial statements in understanding the health of your business, let's focus on other tools available to help you check your business' financial health.

Tools for Determining Your Financial Health

One of the first tools is financial ratios. These ratios are a comparison tool that allow you to judge where your business is now and how it compares to the past, as well as how it compares to other businesses in your industry or economic sector. Here are a few of these key ratios that you could use in your business:

- Liquidity - your current assets divided by your current liabilities
- Profitability - your gross profit divided by your total sales
- Inventory – Average stock multiplied by 365 divided by cost of goods sold (COGS)
- Return on investment – Net profit before tax times 100 divided by equity

All this information is available in your financials and located within your QuickBooks accounting software. Depending on your needs, you can choose the financial ratio that gets you the right information, prior to making the next decisions for your business.

Another tool is intertwined with your business plan, known as a strategic review. Part of this process is updating your business plan. What is a business plan? It is a statement of the goals for your business and how you believe they can be achieved. As you formulate your business plan, consider the needs of your business and who your competitors are. Your business plan can also include addressing key staff roles, as well as your exit plan regarding selling or transitioning your business to new leadership.

It can be a critical tool, not only for the start up of your business, but also for taking stock of where your business is now and areas for growth, both locally and internationally. It helps you to define your business objectives for your employees and investors.

A strategic review takes what you have learned and the changes you want to make, and then applies them to your long-term strategy for your business, as is defined in your business plan. During this process, you can identify oversights or issues negatively impacting the financial health of your business. Once you have that information, you can start to change your plan to resolve the issues and thus improve your outcomes.

It is also a time to revisit the basics of your business. Ask yourself the following questions:

- Is your current strategy working?

- Are your business goals and objectives realistic?
- Has your market or the needs of your customers changed?
- Are there new opportunities available?

As you do this review, you are going to need to dig into your finances, and QuickBooks has the reports and information to help you do so effectively.

Another aspect of understanding your financial health is tied to your sales pipeline. You can look at your customers and determine where they are in the sales pipeline and what potential customers you may have. However, if your pipeline is empty, then you could be losing customers or not marketing effectively to gain new ones. That could prompt a review of your sales tactics.

Throughout this guide, we have frequently mentioned cash flow. Part of evaluating and understanding your financial health is knowing your cash flow, including where money is coming in and where it is going out. Using a cash flow forecast, you can plan ahead to even out spending over the course of a month or quarter. Also, if you are consistently struggling to pay bills and expenses month to month, you may need to put cash savings strategies in place.

A cash flow forecast can be helpful for a small business that deals with irregular or seasonal cash flow. After all, absorbing the highs and lows of cash flow can be difficult if you do not have reserves available to help even it out. Preparing for a cash-flow crisis is to forecast for a specific period and then review your progress against it.

Look at how much you have spent on various items in the past and that can help you to determine how much you are likely to spend on these items in the future. Plus, you can identify any cash inflows, including revenue, interest earnings, and your cash and credit sales. You can also identify the potential cash gaps during the month and prepare contingency measures to still pay your expenses.

You might want to explore a working capital loan based on your accounts receivable or invoices. There are other financing options that can help you to create a cash flow cushion to keep your business running smoothly. A cash flow forecast is also key to exploring how different disasters or a major customer becoming insolvent can impact your business.

As your business grows and changes, you can adjust your forecasts, increasing their accuracy and use them to adjust your strategy for seasonal fluctuations to avoid potential future shortfalls.

Finally, as part of any review of the financial health of your business, take a look at your debts associated with the business. You might need to borrow money for your business from time to time, but if you are operating on debt financing with high interest rates, then you put the health of your business at risk.

However, borrowing money can be helpful in terms of investing in the expansion of your business or updating machinery and hardware. Therefore, as you review your finances, it is important to make strategic choices to avoid overwhelming your business with a large amount of high interest debt.

Another aspect of your financial health is understanding your tax liability and how it can impact your business, which is the topic of the next chapter.

Chapter 4 – Understanding Your Tax Liability

When it comes to running a business, there are going to be taxes that need to be paid. Depending on your business, you may have to collect sales tax and pay income and property taxes. There are going to be taxes that relate to your local county or city, as well as state and federal taxes. Each of these are going to require you to make payments, typically on a quarterly basis. Plus, when you file your annual tax return, you are less likely to have additional penalties relating to your tax bill, because of your timely quarterly payments.

QuickBooks assists in not only recording the tax payments you've made, but also in estimating your tax payments and helping you to determine what deductions apply based on your business expenses, plus the bookkeeping benefits of this software.

Tracking Business Expenses to Determine Deductions

As you input your business expenses, you are going to be able to categorize them. QuickBooks allows you to choose the category, but also allows you to create categorizing rules that mean new entries will automatically be categorized. For those who are doing their own bookkeeping, as part of the administration of running your business, you can save time through the various methods offered by QuickBooks to input and categorize your expenses.

One of the methods that QuickBooks offers to track expenses is to connect your bank accounts, credit cards, PayPal account, Square account, and more to your accounting software. QuickBooks will then import and categorize expenses as they occur, creating an automatic system for recording expenses and income. You can also review all those expenses and then create rules that will allow for this process to be completed automatically. Once you take this step, you will be able to run expense reports letting you see how all the money in your business is being spent.

You can also benefit from the snapping and saving of photos of receipts, which can then be loaded into QuickBooks. There is the added benefit of being able to sync QuickBooks across your phone, tablet, and computer to keep your accounting data up to date. Another benefit is that you can save space, because your receipts can also be scanned into the software as you incur them.

Once it's tax time, your deductions will be easier to identify, simply because you have automatically sorted all your income and expenses through the accounting software. You also have the advantage of QuickBooks tailoring the tax categories to be just right for your business type. Depending on your business needs, you can also create tax categories to get more specific, although this option is not available with the QuickBooks Self-Employed version.

Now that you are getting a better understanding of how QuickBooks can record your income and expenses; it is important to learn how the accounting software calculates your estimated tax payments.

Estimating Tax Payments with QuickBooks

Determining your estimated tax payments is going to involve different information as part of the calculations depending on your business, particularly for those who are self-employed.

As a self-employed individual, there are three different aspects that are the basis of calculating estimated tax payments. First, there is your self-employment income and deductions, which is the revenue and the deductions that you can take as part of your work. Next, there are the projections of your self-employed income and deductions, which are anticipated to occur over the calendar year. Finally, there is the tax bracket that you fall into, along with the other information that you added to your tax profile during the initial setup of your accounting software.

Projections can arguably be the least defined part of the equation. In order to estimate your quarterly tax payments, a projection is necessary, which is essentially a logical guess of your yearly profit. To create that logical guess, your current income and deductions are factored to-gether to figure the profit. Then the accounting software averages it and projects it forward for the remainder of the year.

These projections can get more accurate as the year progresses, be-cause now real-time information is being factored into the projection. You also have the added benefit of checking the actual data and ad-justing it through the Quarterly Estimated Taxes option.

Your tax bracket is based on your income level and set by the govern-ment. Your answers to the general questions during setup regarding your financial circumstances are going to help the software determine what tax bracket you land in. The software also adjusts for income that may have already been taxed, such as income from a W-2 employee, as well as giving you the standard deduction.

As a self-employed individual, you might be looking at those estimated tax payments and wondering why they are so high. First, there is the fact that you are projecting profit for the entire year, which includes not just the income you have already received, but the potential income you anticipate making for the remainder of the year.

Part of the reason that these estimated payments are also higher is that you are paying both the Social Security and Medicare taxes, serv-ing as the employer and employee. If you were a W-2 employee, then you are going to only pay half of those taxes, because your employer pays the other half.

Another factor to keep in mind is that if you are not up to date with re-viewing your transactions, then you might be missing deductions, which means your profit, projections, and estimates are higher. The goal is to owe no taxes for your self-employment work by the end of the year. Paying throughout the year will mean that you don't have a huge tax bill when you file your taxes because you have already paid them, similar to a traditional withholding found on a paycheck.

To find your quarterly taxes and estimated payments, go to the naviga-tion bar, then click on taxes and select Quarterly Taxes, where you can find your quarterly schedule, recommended payment totals, and any payments that were already credited. If you click on any specific quar-ter, you can reveal the details related to that quarter income, profit, deductions, and tax payments. On the right-hand side, you can view the projected profits for the remainder of the year, along with the details of your tax profile.

You can also look at your whole year to find your biggest deductions. Click on Taxes and then Annual Taxes to see your taxable business profit and details about your expenses, as well as how they translate into your deductions. If you want a tax summary or tax details, then you can download a PDF of this information, which makes it a great way to transport that information to your accountant or as part of filing your taxes.

Keep in mind that QuickBooks does not calculate more complicated tax scenarios or other types of tax estimates, such as:

- State income taxes
- Sales tax
- Alternative Minimum Tax (AMT)
- Medical expenses, stock payouts, and 401(K) draws
- One-time lump sum distributions
- Tax credits

If you do not make your estimated tax payments, then you risk being penalized by the IRS. Individuals and corporations, which should be filing quarterly taxes and don't, can be penalized by as much as 5% for every month the payment is late, but it cannot exceed the total payment due. Penalties can also be applied for the underpayment of estimated taxes.

Part of the reason these payments are so important is because federal income taxes are paid as you go. If you don't have wages that withholding taxes can be taken from, then it is up to you to pay estimated taxes four times a year, on April 15, June 17, September 16, and January 15. Doing so should cover your tax bill.

Therefore, it is important to keep your bookkeeping up to date, to be sure that your estimated tax payments are as accurate as possible. By monitoring your income and expenses throughout the year, then you can adjust your payments, increasing them where necessary to avoid underpayment penalties.

Changes in Business Income – Minor fluctuations in your business are not going to affect your estimated taxes, but a significant change can affect your remaining payments.

Changes in Personal Circumstances – A marriage, divorce, birth, or adoption can impact your tax liability and estimated payments.

New Tax Laws – As the recent changes in tax law for 2018 filings demonstrates, when tax laws are changed, it can impact what you might owe and how much. Using QuickBooks, which is updated to reflect these changes in tax law, you can make estimated payments to reflect estimated tax liability.

It can be challenging to have the cash on hand for your tax payments. Working with your accounting software, you can use your knowledge of your cash flow to put money aside for your estimated payments, making them earlier if necessary, to make sure that they are made. It can even be helpful to put the tax funds in a separate account for that purpose.

The tax forms and schedules that you need to complete are going to be based on your business tax structure. Working with QuickBooks, you can understand your potential tax liability and make estimated payments accordingly.

Throughout this chapter, the focus has been on the practical aspects of QuickBooks as it relates to your tax liability. Now let's focus on how you can add the option to use QuickBooks for your payroll needs.

Chapter 5 – Options for Payroll and Timekeeping

The idea of payroll and the calculations needed have gotten a bad rap, and many business owners shudder at the idea of handling payroll on their own. Many have opted to pay an accounting service to handle payroll for them. However, with the rise of direct deposit and automated tax payments, a business owner no longer needs to worry about creating a traditional paper payroll.

Instead, there are online options available that allow you to run your payroll, direct deposit employees' checks, give them an online viewing option, file your tax forms and make tax payments, all from a simple interface and at a budget-friendly price. Let's learn about the payroll options available through QuickBooks for both its online and desktop versions.

Payroll Through QuickBooks Online

QuickBooks online versions offer the means to handle payroll through an add-on, thus allowing you to run your weekly or bi-weekly payroll with a few clicks. To begin, you need to add each of your employees to the system, including their social security number, address, birth date, start date, how frequently they will be paid, their withholding information, and their pay rate. After all the information is in the system, you can then start running payroll, using either paper checks or direct deposit.

How does it work? To start, you simply go to the navigation bar on your left, choose employees and follow all the prompts. QuickBooks is user-friendly, meaning that you can easily follow the steps to add employees and run your payroll.

Once the pay period is over, go into each employee and enter their hours for that period (for more information about timekeeping and tracking employees' hours, go to TimeKeeping and Tracking Labor Costs under this chapter). Since Payroll for QuickBooks Online is web-based, you can access the latest federal and state payroll tax rates and forms for your tax withholding calculations. The program will instantly calculate your federal and state payroll taxes and remind you about when and how much you owe. Although you can still write a check and send it in as a payment of your taxes, today QuickBooks offers the option to pay your federal, as well as select state taxes, electronically using E-Pay.

This add-on allows you to avoid entering data twice, because it can easily be integrated with your QuickBooks financial data. Additionally, all your data is being constantly backed up through their online system. You also do not have to wait for updates as with traditional software. As the owner, you can also easily share data and work with others. This option allows you to give your accountant access to all your payroll data.

Once you sign up, QuickBooks offers a step-by-step guide for setting up your payroll, including adding prior payroll data as needed. Setting up direct deposit can take a little longer but can be an effective way to manage payroll and give your employees access to their funds right away on payday. QuickBooks also offers dedicated phone support from 6 am to 6 pm Pacific time, as well as 24/7 online support.

When it comes to using the online versions, the same subscription options apply, so you can choose the payroll add-on subscription that works for you. Keep in mind, you do not have to wait till the beginning of the year to start working with Payroll Online. In fact, their support team can walk you through importing data from your previous payroll system.

Your business might not have previously had employees, but as your business has grown, then you might need to add personnel to meet its needs. Perhaps your business already has employees, but you have been using one of the desktop versions of QuickBooks. You may be wondering if you can access a payroll option.

QuickBooks Payroll Services for Desktop Versions

To start with, QuickBooks does offer a subscription payroll service that enables payroll on your Desktop version. There are three options available, the Basic, Enhanced, or Assisted Payroll. There was a Standard version, but it is no longer offered. Those existing subscribers who already have this version will continue to receive support. It is also important to note that their payroll service is not available with QuickBooks Mac. This information could factor into your decision regarding which QuickBooks desktop version that you opt to use for your business.

A benefit of using QuickBooks Payroll Service is that you can export these transactions right into your QuickBooks accounting software, making it a seamless integration. If you opt out of the QuickBooks Desktop Payroll Services, you can still set up a manual payroll, however, the software will not do the calculations for you. While you must then do the payroll calculations yourself, QuickBooks does offer a free online Payroll Calculator.

What Is Offered in the Payroll Service?

Here is a list of the options available through QuickBooks Payroll Service, although the specific options included in your subscription will depend on the version that you choose.

Payroll Updates – Provide the most current and accurate rates and calculations for supported state and federal tax tables, payroll tax forms, and e-file and pay options.

Create Paychecks – Create and print paychecks with automatic tax calculations. Nominal usage fee may apply. To create a paycheck, do the following:

1. From the left menu, select Workers, then Employee.

2. Select run Payroll.

3. Select your payroll schedule.

4. Select the names of the employees that belong to that schedule.

5. Enter their hours and amounts owed (if using TSheets, import that information in from the cloud).

6. Select Preview and then submit.

7. Select Print paycheck and print pay stubs. If you use ViewMy-Paycheck, then this information will be made available to your

employees through that system.

Direct Deposit for Employees/1099 Contractors – You can deposit an employee's payroll right into their checking or savings account. There may be per-transaction or per-payroll fees associated with the transmission of the funds. To enroll in Direct Deposit, complete the following:

1. Go to the Employees menu, select My Payroll Services, then Activate Direct Deposit.
2. In the Verify Your Company Information section:
   - Select Edit.
   - Determine which industry matches your business the best and select it.
   - Enter your email address, Social Security Number or business EIN, and birthday.
   - Make any changes to your Payroll Administrator and confirm the email address.
   - Enter the information of the account to be debited for fees, as well as funding your employees' paychecks and other transactions.
3. Click on View Agreement and confirm your agreement.
4. Answer the questions provided under your Check Security Limits.
5. Submit and print the confirmation page, along with the instructions provided.

Before your direct deposit add-on can be used, you must confirm your banking information, set up each employee's bank information in the software, and then create paychecks for direct deposit. There are three types of checks in the payroll service, unscheduled, scheduled, and termination. Once you set up a scheduled payroll, you can group employees based on their payroll schedule, but verify the schedule dates before running your payroll.

ViewMyPaycheck – This option allows employees to view and print their checks 24/7 through an online interface. You no longer accrue the costs associated with check stubs and mailing them. Employees can now print them or save them on their own.

E-File or E-Pay – These options allow you to avoid mailing forms and payments to state and federal agencies. The benefit is that you have a means to track payment and it can be credited to your accounts faster than traditional mailing of your forms and payments.

Intuit Workers' Comp Payment Service – By combining your workers' comp with your payroll system, Workers' Compensation Payment Service will automatically pay your Workers' Comp premiums using your payroll data.

After the Fact Payroll – This option allows your accountant to enter, verify, and adjust after-the-fact paychecks from a single spreadsheet-style screen. Other options are also available that include tools that are specifically for an accountant to use.

It must be noted that while you can have multiple employees in Quick-Books, you may have fees for each employee that is part of your payroll. Depending on your subscription, that fee could be accessed per pay period or on a monthly basis. QuickBooks payroll services can experience performance issues if you have more than 800 employees in the system.

Now that you know about some of the payroll options available, below is information about the type of payroll service versions and which options they offer.

Basic

The Basic option gives you payroll updates, allows you to create paychecks, utilize direct deposit for employees and 1099 contractors, put ViewMyPaycheck in place for your employees, receive email notification of critical notices, access Intuit Workers' Comp Payment Service, and free expert support.

Enhanced

The Enhanced option includes everything from the Basic option, along with access to Federal and State forms, as well as E-File and E-Pay. This option gives you the ability to make your payroll tax payments and file your payroll tax forms electronically.

There is also an Enhanced Version for Accountants, which includes after-the-fact payroll. You can also complete tax forms for clients using Basic Payroll. There is an auto-fill option for your paid preparer information and if they file as your reporting agent. All these options allow you to streamline your payroll activities, making it easier to handle in house and thus reduce your costs.

Assisted

The Assisted version includes everything from the Enhanced version, but also includes the option for Intuit to file and pay your taxes for you and a no tax penalties guarantee.

Time Keeping and Tracking Labor Costs

As you can see, the Payroll Services can help you to handle this task and automate it. Another aspect that employers want to track is employees' hours. TSheets through QuickBooks allows you to use cloud-based time tracking, getting rid of written timesheets for payroll. You can also run payroll faster, because all the information for payroll is already in the system, so there is less that must be imputed.

Not only is there the benefit of saving time on the days that you run payroll, you can also be more accurate in billing time to customers for labor. You can create, update, and manage employee schedules and send alerts to keep them up to date. Using a mobile app, you can allow employees to clock in and clock out, take breaks, and track time on specific jobs without coming back into the office or wasting time in line waiting for the time clock.

TSheets can also give you the ability to see where employees are using the GPS function, keeping better track of your mobile workforce. It can also be a great way to create better processes to reduce wasted time in various areas of your business. You can also run reports in real time to understand your labor costs in real time. Finally, TSheets offers the ability to automate employee overtime rates, and put limits in place to keep your overtime costs down.

There are monthly and annual subscription plans available, with a fee for each user along with a base fee. The system can support up to 99 users, although QuickBooks does offer plans for larger companies.

As you can see, QuickBooks offers a variety of options to meet the needs of businesses in all stages of their development. Picking the right options will depend largely on what your business needs and the type of work done. After all, you might be less interested in inventory options if your business is service-oriented and carries no real inventory.

Now it is important to sit down with your business plan and determine your needs. The next chapter will go into what you need to think about before choosing the right accounting service software for your business.

Chapter 6 – Deciding What is Right for You

Setting up your business is an amazing process, one that includes managing a variety of details. You must handle the production of your goods or services, delivery of goods or services, marketing, managing employees, addressing the needs of your customers, tracking income and expenses, as well as creating the processes and procedures that will help your business run.

Part of the process of setting up your business is finding a way to manage all your financial information effectively without it dominating your administration tasks, and that means choosing the right accounting service software to compliment your business needs. While there are a variety of services and software available, it is important to choose one that can grow with your business, allowing you to upgrade as needed.

QuickBooks is an accounting service software that allows you to automate bookkeeping tasks which are the basis of all the financial information for your business. It can provide a variety of options and versions, making it possible to find what you need for your business with ease. Plus, as your business grows, there are upgrade options that allow you to add what you need when you need it.

It is important to note that many of the options available through Quick-Books can be accessed through its mobile applications, giving you the ability to categorize or input transactions when you are on the go. For individuals who are self-employed, these mobile functions can be a way to minimize how much time you spend inputting transactions at the end of a business trip or function, since you can do it in the moment.

Other applications through QuickBooks are customized to be useful for small to medium-sized businesses, giving you the ability to match your business to the right software version. There are other benefits to using QuickBooks accounting service software, particularly as it relates to accessing capital for expanding your business and funding capital investments.

Use QuickBooks to Apply for Financing

Even applying for additional financing can be done through Quick-Books Capital, using the financial data that you already have available in your QuickBooks, making the application process fast and easy. So, what is QuickBooks Capital?

It is a service offered by Intuit Financing, Inc., which provides business loans to eligible QuickBooks clients. Using a holistic viewpoint, Quick-Books Capital looks to create funding options that are right for your business. There are two different funding options available:

- Directly underwriting loans
- Providing a marketplace to explore and be matched with curated lenders

For those individuals who use QuickBooks Online, you can apply for and receive short-term working capital loans. Factors that can impact your qualification for funding include past business history, your use of QuickBooks Online, personal and business credit history, and your current liabilities.

Generally, QuickBooks Capital requires a FICO score of 580, no personal or business bankruptcies in the past two years, and at least $50,000 in revenue over the past year. There are also businesses on the prohibited business list, so you need to make sure your business is not on that list prior to applying. Each application is viewed individually, so there is some discretion and not everyone meeting the basic application criteria will receive a loan.

The Capital Marketplace allows you to shop loan terms, lines of credit, and more. You can see your options without impacting your credit score and select the right funding option for your needs. At that point, you will have to complete the lending process with your selected financing partner.

Even if you are going through a more traditional financing option, your QuickBooks financial statements can be used as part of your application process. There are a variety of uses and benefits to using Quick-Books as your accounting service software.

Determining What Is Right For Your Business

Throughout this guide, the focus has been on introducing you to all the options and versions offered by QuickBooks. It gives you the ability to customize your accounting software to meet the needs of your business now, but also in the future as you continue to grow. Along the way, you have learned about the various offerings, which are targeted for businesses that are just starting out, self-employed individuals, and even medium-sized businesses with a number of employees.

What makes QuickBooks appealing is that you can access services through its online platform, allowing you to know that your data is constantly being backed up, which means you don't have to worry about it being lost if your hardware should fail or your server were to go down for any unexpected reason. For small businesses, having the means to back up their financial data is key to allowing their business to survive and thrive even after a disaster, such as a tornado, flood, or fire.

Your business plan should include a disaster plan and the means to access your data, possibly from another location. With QuickBooks software being available in five online versions, you can have the peace of mind that comes from knowing your data is not lost just because your building or business location suffered damage.

However, QuickBooks also offers options for those who prefer to keep their software in house, with desktop versions. It should also be noted that these versions can allow you to give access to your business accountant, making it easy for you to transfer financial information each quarter and during tax season.

To determine the best option for your business, ask yourself these critical questions:

- Am I self-employed, a sole proprietor, a limited liability company (LLC), or a Corporation?

- Will I have employees? If so, how many?

- Do I want to use timekeeping software, or do I prefer a handwritten timekeeping method for my employees?

- Are my employees going to be mobile or will they be located primarily in our main office or production facility?

- Will I be doing my bookkeeping in house or is it being completed by an accountant?

- What is my budget for accounting software?

- Do I need regular updates and regular access to support for my software?

- Would I prefer a one-time cost or a subscription with a monthly or annual fee?

- Will I need financing or working capital?

- Do I have a business plan?

- What is my projected growth? Am I looking to expand my business into new markets?

All these questions can help you to determine the type of QuickBooks software you need and whether an online or desktop version will work for you. As part of your decision-making process, it is important to weigh the costs involved. While the monthly subscription cost for the Self-Employed Online Version is under $20, other versions of QuickBooks can come at a much greater cost.

For instance, using the payroll option could mean incurring costs per employee, a base cost for the service, and additional costs for direct deposit or filing of tax forms and payments. While these costs might seem small at first, they could become more of a budget buster as your business grows. Therefore, it is important to keep in mind that you can move up to a version that offers more options as part of the base subscription price to offset some costs.

It is important to note that you can contact QuickBooks to customize your experience and allow their trained staff to help you find the right options for your needs. They are going to focus on what your business needs now. Still, as your business grows, keep in mind that QuickBooks can grow with it.

Another aspect is that QuickBooks does a variety of calculations for you automatically. Individuals who use Excel spreadsheets find themselves working harder to determine the right calculations. As a business owner, time is money. Recognize that your time is valuable and the more of it you must spend on your bookkeeping, the less time you have to get out there and make money by connecting with your customers and generating sales by meeting their needs.

For someone who is self-employed, your hourly rate may be $40. If you spend three hours a week working on a spreadsheet, then you have lost $120 of revenue. Using QuickBooks software can save you those three hours, thus giving you the opportunity to gain $120 in revenue for your business. Now that $20 a month for the subscription seems worth the cost. It is about understanding the value of your time as a business owner and choosing the right tools to give you value added benefits.

Granted, not every subscription is going to have the same monthly cost, but it is important to weigh those costs versus the benefits you receive from the software itself.

By opting for an accounting service software, you can cut the bookkeeping time down and give yourself more time to focus on growing your business and creating new opportunities to meet the needs of your customers. This guide is meant to help you better understand what QuickBooks has to offer and how it can be of benefit to your business. No matter if you are just starting out or are ready to move away from tracking expenses on a spreadsheet, QuickBooks can offer you the right fit. Exploring their options can be the first step in taking your business to a new and exciting level!

Made in the USA
Monee, IL
04 April 2023

31345177R00065